Dedicated to

Dr. D. S. Kotnis (柯棣华大夫)

(1910-1942)

Quick & Easy

Way To Learn Chinese

Dr. Yukeshwar Kumar

Reader, Department of East Asian Studies

University of Delhi

Qualis Books

G T BOOK AGENCY

ISBN : 81-87838-06-X
ISBN : 9788187838036

Reprinted 2026

Quick & Easy Way to Learn Chinese

Published by
Qualis Books
140, Medha Apartment
Mayur Vihar, Ext. Phase 1,
New Delhi - 110091
E-mail : qualisbooks@yahoo.co.in

Printed in India at
D.K. Fine Art Press
New Delhi.

About the Author

Dr. Yukteshwar Kumar (余德烁博士), Reader in Chinese, Department of East Asian Studies, University of Delhi is one of the youngest Readers of independent India. Apart from teaching for more than 14 years at JNU, Visva-Bharati, Santiiketan and now at University of Delhi, he has authored several articles on China and Sino-Indian Relations. He has also authored a book titled *A History of Sino-Indian Relations: 1st Century AD to 7th Century AD*. Dr. Kumar has also visited China several times for participating in seminars and conferences. He has been awarded several scholarships including the prestigious Nehru Fellowship. Apart from working at AIR, Delhi during his students days, he has been also involved in doing interpretation at national and international level. He also had the honor of doing interpretation for Mrs. Sonia Gandhi Ji, The Governor and Chief Minister of Bihar, the Chinese Foreign Minister and the Chief Justice of India and China.

Ankit (安吉德), one of the brightest and upcoming young scholar on China has been actively participating in national and international conferences. He has been also awarded several scholarships and won several quiz and debate competition at both college and university level.

Acknowledgment

"Quick and Easy Way to Learn Chinese" as the title itself suggests, is written keeping in mind the people who have no knowledge of Chinese. Learning Chinese will not only boost the employment opportunities in the field of business, trade, education, tourism etc. but would also help in providing an upper hand as it is a growing belief that 21st century belongs to China. Thus, this book is aimed for those who want to speak Chinese in their day-to-day life in the shortest time possible. However, as far as script and writing characters is concerned, it is not explained in detailed manner, as character writing is not taken up in this book, because of the paucity of space and time.

This book is basically divided into four parts. The first part, 'Introduction to Chinese', which deals with the Tones, Initials and Finals etc. is the most important one. It is highly recommended that Initals, Finals, Tones and Sounds should be read aloud repeatedly as it forms the base of Spoken Chinese. The second part basically deals with the 'Chinese Grammar', which is again the second most important part in learning this language. The third and fourth parts comprised of 'General Vocabulary' and 'Conversational Chinese' respectively. The 'General Vocabulary' is written in English, Pinyin and its equivalent Chinese characters, so that one cannot find any hardships in pronouncing them. Then the fourth part, which is of 'Conversational Chinese', is comprised of simple and authentic Chinese sentences, which one can use in his or her trips to China. This part also has the detailed political state structure of China as well as the names of major countries of the world in English, *pinyin* and Chinese characters. The sentences in each text have been arranged in three lines with English sentences, *Romanization* and equivalent Chinese characters.

In the book, we have used the modern *Pinyin* system, which is commonly used in China. At some places, for the benefit of the readers we have devided the dysyllabic Chinese Pinyin words into two separate monosyllabic words.

We would also like to take this opportunity to convey our heartfelt thanks to Prof. Sreemati Chakrobarty, Prof. Priyadarshi Mukherjee, Dr.Anita Sharma, Mr. K.C. Mathur, Mr. Liang Yadong, visiting teacher from China and Ms. Shreeparna Roy from the Department of East Asian Studies, University of Delhi. Without the sincere support of all these teachers, colleagues, friends and family members, this volume of "Quick and Easy Way to learn Chinese" would have not been possible.

Dr. Yukteshwar Kumar

Ankit

CONTENTS

Part-3

Part-4

Foreword

Learning Chinese is a new fashion today as it is highly rewarding and soon becoming a global language. Chinese is already a UN language and more and more people are today making painstaking efforts to grasp this language. A very successful American entrepreneur has kept a Chinese maid to look after his daughter so that she could start speaking Chinese as fluently as possible and as early as possible.

Sino-Indian trade has already surpassed the 20 billion USD mark in 2006 and it is expected to touch 40 Billion USD by 2010. Relation between India and China has been already revived after it touched a nadir in 1962. 1962 war should be seen as a very small dark-spot in the long friendly history of more than 2,000 years between the two nations. Not only business entrepreneurs and high government officials are frequenting each other countries but common people are also visiting each other's countries on pleasure trip. However, language still remains a constrain as common person in China hardly speak good English and anybody going to China on whatever trip must learn a few words of Chinese.

Introduction

Chinese is spoken by the highest number of people in the world. Apart from People's Republic of China, this language is also spoken in several other countries and regions like Singapore, Malaysia, Indonesia, Thailand, Hongkong, Macao and Taiwan.

The Chinese are the largest single ethnic (Han) group in the world, therefore the official Chinese language that is 'Mandarin' is spoken by more people than any other language. According to the recent BBC report, more than 52% of Chinese speak mandarin. Chinese is also one of the world's oldest language, its written records stretching back to more than 3,500 years.

Many people imagine Chinese would be a very difficult language to learn and indeed it was, till *'Wade and Giles'* system was practiced and now with the introduction of *'Pinyin'* system, it has become comparatively easier to grasp the language. Spoken Chinese is not as difficult as one had thought – One may find it comparatively easy! The written language is totally different from spoken one, which we will deal later in the book.

Part-1

The Chinese Language

Many of us have already heard of the term 'Mandarin' or 'Mandarin Chinese' which is declared as the official language for China. This refers to the northern dialect, which is spoken by over 52% of the Chinese or Han people and has become the *lingua franca* for the whole of China. This National language is known as *pǔtōnghuà* or 'common speech' (普通话). North-eastern pronunciation *dōngběi huà* (东北话) is taken as the standard but there are many regional variations, some not easy to grasp with. *Pǔtōnghuà* or 'common speech' (普通话) is taught in schools and used in colleges and universities all over the China. The majority of TV and radio program as well as films are also made in *pǔtōnghuà*. You will be glad to know that the Chinese language, we are going to study in this book will be *pǔtōnghuà* or 'common speech' (普通话). Hence, it will enable you to converse with the majority of Chinese people in the world.

Romanization

The written language does not have a phonetic alphabet but various systems have been devised for transcribing Chinese sound into the Latin script. The standard form in use today is known as *pīnyīn* or 'spell sound' (拼音), which was adopted as the official system of the People's Republic of China in 1958. It has been now universally adopted worldwide. *Pīnyīn* is used as a tool to teach the correct pronunciation of the Chinese language to the children starting elementary Chinese before they have mastered enough characters.

Sounds and tones General Introduction

There are just over 400 basic monosyllables in Chinese, which seems an incredibly small number and must be the result of sound-simplification over a few thousand years. But the difficulty is compounded somewhat by the fact that Chinese is a tonal language. There are four tones in *pǔtōnghuà*, so by multiplying 400 by four we get a total of approximately 1600 separate items, although not all basic sounds exist in all four tones. The other way is by combining two syllables with a similar meaning into one 'word'. For example, *ài* and *qíng* mean 'love' and 'feelings' respectively and could be confused with other 'words', if used separately, but together they can only mean 'love' *àiqíng*. This makes communication considerably easier all around.

What we mean by 'syllable' in Chinese is usually composed of an initial and a final. The initial, if there is one, is a consonant at the beginning of the syllable and the final is the rest of the syllable, e.g. 'hang' in which '*h*' is the initial and '*ang*' is the final.

Initials

Modern Chinese has 23 initials including 'W' and 'Y', which some people regard as semi-vowels. These can be divided into three sounds. Aspirated which means that the air is puffed out strongly when you make these sounds, but not when you make an unaspirated one. Voiceless means that the vocal chords do not vibrate.

Table of Initials

Chinese Phonetic	Alphabet English Key Words/ Sounds
B	as p in 's**p**ike', unaspirated
P	as p in '**p**itch', aspirated
M	as m in '**m**an'
F	as f in '**f**ish'
D	as in 'straigh**t**', unaspirated
T	as in '**t**ouch', aspirated
N	as n in '**n**ice'
L	as in '**l**amp'
G	as k in 's**k**ill', unaspirated
K	as k in '**k**angaroo'
H	as h in '**h**oly'
J	'**ch**eck'. The closest match is as j in 'a**j**ar', unaspirated
Q	as ch in '**ch**urch', aspirated

X	as sh in '**sh**irt'
Zh	as j in '**j**eep', but end smoothly with 'r' sound, unaspirated
Ch	as ch in '**ch**in' but end smoothly with 'r' sound, unaspirated
Sh	as sh in '**sh**arp' but end smoothly with 'r' sound, unaspirated
R	as r in '**r**ank', but with the lips spread and with the tongue curled upwards
Z	it is halfway between 'be**ds**' and 'be**ts**', unaspirataed
C	as ts in 'ca**ts**', unaspirated
S	as s in '**s**un'
Y	as y in '**y**ear'
W	as w in '**w**ay'

Finals

There are 36 finals in Chinese. A final is a simple or compound vowel or a vowel plus a nasal consonant. A few 'syllables' may have no initial consonant but every one has to have a vowel.

Tables of Finals

Finals	English Key Words/Sounds
A	as a in 'f**a**ther'
O	as a in 'r**aw**'
E	as I 'st**ir**'
Ai	as '**eye**', but a bit lighter
Ei	as ey in 'h**ey**'
Ao	as ow in'c**ow**', a is much more audible than o
Ou	as ow in '**owl**'
An	as aun in '**aun**ty', front Nasal sound
En	as en in 'tak**en**', front Nasal sound

Ang	as ong in 'l**ong**', rear Nasal sound
Eng	as ung in 'l**ung**', rear Nasal sound
ong	As **u** + **eng**; starts with the vowel sound in 'b**oo**k' and end with the velar nasal sound in s**ing**
ia	as y in '**ya**rd'
ie	as yie in slang word '**yeh**'
iao	as **i** + **ou**
ian	as **i** + **an**, like '**yen**'
in	as **i** + **en**, front Nasal sound
iang	as **i** + **ang**
ing	as **i** + **eng**, rear Nasal sound
iong	as **ü** + **eng**
u	as oo in '**pooh**'
ua	as **u** + **a**
uo	as **u** + **o**, the o is pronounced shorter and lighter than in the o final
uai	as **u** + **ai**

uei	as **u** + **ei**, here, the I is pronounced like ei
uan	as **u** + **an**
uen	as **u** + **en**, like the on in the English 'w**on**'
uang	as **u** + **ang**, like the ang in '**ang**er'
ueng	as **u** + **eng**, starts with the vowel sound in 'b**oo**k' and ends with the velar nasal sound in 's**ing**'
ü	to get this sound, say 'ee' with rounded lips
üe	as ü+ **e**, the u is short and light
üan	as ü+ **an**
ün	as ü + **en**
er	exists on its own, or as last part of final in combination

Tones in Mandarin Chinese

Chinese is a tonal language. In Mandarin Chinese, there are four tones, indicated respectively by the tone marks —,/, ∨ and \.

Tone	Tone mark	Description	Example
First tone	—	high, level pitch	tī 踢 = kick
Second tone	/	starting high and rising	tí 提 = lift
Third tone	∨	falling first, then rising	tǐ 体 = body
Fourth tone	\	falling	tì 替 = replace

As can be seen from the fourth column above, the tone is marked above the vowel on the romanized syllable. It is marked only in the *pinyin* romanization, not on the characters. Some words have unstressed syllables. These are toneless, and are not given tone marks. For example, in *wǒmen* 我们 (= we, us), the syllable *men* is toneless and therefore has no tone mark on it. This type of syllable is often called a neutral tone syllable.

Tone Changes

Sometimes the tone of a syllable or a word changes according to the syllable that follows it.

Measure Words

Liàng cí -量词: Measure Word

In Chinese, a numeral cannot quantify a noun by itself. It has to be accompanied by the measure word that is appropriate for the noun that is being used. Each noun has a specific measure word or set of measure words that can be used with it. In expressions of quantification, the numeral comes first, followed by the measure word and the noun. Below is a list of commonly used measure words, along with descriptions of the types of nouns for which they are used.

Measure word	What it modifies	Example
Bǎ（把）	Chair, Key, Knife	sān **bǎ** yi zi (Three chairs)
Běn（本）	Book, Magazine, Dictionary etc.	yī **běn** shū

		(A book)
Bǐ (笔)	for sums of money	nà **bi** qián (That sum of money)
Fēng (封)	Letters, Telegrams	zhè **fēng** xìn (This letter)
Gè (个)	This is the most common Measure word. It is handy to use if one does not know the specific measure word	yí **gè** rén (A person) liăng **gè** wèntí (Two questions)
Jià (架)	Aero planes, Cameras, Pianos.	wu **jià** fēijī (Five Aeroplanes)
Jiàn (件)	Luggage, Clothes, Furniture etc.	nà **jiàn** xíngli (That luggage)
Jié (节)	Section, Period, Segment	liăng **jié** kè (Two periods)

Jù（句）	A sentence, units of speech, poetry	liù **jù** shī (Six lines of poem)
Kē（棵）	Trees, Plants	bā **kē** shù (Eight trees)
Kǒu（口）	Number of people on the family	jiu **kou** rén (Nine people)
Kuài（块）	Money, Soap, bread	sān **kuài** měi yuán (Three USD)
Liàng（辆）	Cars, bikes, lorries	zhè **liàng** qìchē (This car)
Liè（列）	Train	yī **liè** huǒchē (A train)
Qún（群）	Group, crowd, herd or flock	yī **qún** niǎo (A group of birds)

Shuāng (双)	Pairs such as shoes, chopsticks, etc.	liǎng **shuāng** xiē (Two pairs of shoes)
Tái (台)	Machines	liǎng **tái** jìsuànjī (A calculator)
Tiáo (条)	Long, linear objects	sān **tiáo** jiē (Three roads)
Tóu (头)	For certain animals	wǔ **tóu** niú (Five cows)
Wèi (位)	Gentleman, lady, teacher, professor	zhè **wèi** lǎoshīmen (Thease teachers)
Xiàng (项)	Work, task, projects, requirements	yī **xiàng** gōng zuò (A piece of task)

Zhāng (张)	Paper, paintings, tables, maps, etc.	liăng **zhāng** zhuōzi (Two tables)
Zhī (支)	For stick like things-pen, candle, flute	shí **zhī** qiānbi (Ten pencils)
Zhŏng (种)	Kind, sort, type	liăng **zhŏng** rén (Two kind of people)
Zuŏ (座)	Mountains, buildings, structures	nà **zuŏ** shān (That mountain)

Part-2

Grammatical Patterns

Basic Sentence Structure

The basic Chinese sentences are very much similar to that of English sentences. The basic structure of both the languages are Subject + Verb + Object. For example:

1. He watches Television.
   Tā kàn diànshì.
   他看电视。

Here also *Tā* is subject, *kàn* is verb and *diànshì* is object.

Pronouns, Singulars and Plurals

Plural forms are the singular form plus the syllable *men*（们）

I	*Wǒ*	我
We	*Wǒmen*	我们
You	*Nǐ*	你
You (respect)	*Nǐn*	您

You (pl.)	*Nǐmen*	你们
He	*Tā*	他
They	*Tāmen*	他们
She	*Tā*	她
They	*Tāmen*	她们

* In Chinese the *Tā* is used to denote both sexes, but the written form is different from each other as mentioned above.

Equational verb *is, are, am, to be.*

是 (*shì*), is the equational verb 'to be' can be used as the English is, are, am. It can only be used to equate combinations of Nouns, Nouns phrases, and Prononuns. 是 (shì) is not used with Adjectives as it is in English. 是 (shì) is negated when preceded by 不 (bù). 不 (bù) is normally 4th tone, but changes to a 2nd tone when it precedes another 4th tone. For example:

1. We are students.
   wǒmen shì xuésheng.
   我们是学生。

2. They are not students
tāmen bú shì *xuésheng*.
她们不是学生。

Structural particle - *My, mine, his, her, your etc.*
When a noun or a pronoun is used as an attributive to show possession, the structural particle 的 (*de*) must be inserted between attributive and what it qualifies. For example:

1. He is my friend.
tā shì wǒde péngyou.
他是我的朋友。

2. My friend is very good.
wǒde péngyou hénhǎo.
我的朋友很好。

Interrogative Sentences
Questions are formed in Chinese by adding 吗 (*ma*) at the end of the declarative sentences. 什么 (*shénme*), 谁 (*shéi*), 哪儿 (*nǎr*), 怎么样 (*zěnmeyàng*), 为什么(*wéi shénme*), 几 (*jǐ*), 多少 (*duōshǎo*) etc. are some other questions words, that are used to make Interrogative sentences. For example:

1. Are you Mr. Wang?
nǐ shì Wáng xiānsheng ma?
你是王先生吗？

2. Who is she?
tā shì shéi?
她 是谁？

3. Where are you going?
nǐ qù nǎr?
你去哪儿？

Affirmative Plus Negative Questions

Juxtaposing the affirmative form and negative form of the main element of the predicate can make affirmative plus negative questions. For example:

1. Are they not your friend?
tāmen shìbùshì nǐde péngyou?
他们是不是你的朋友？

2. Yes. They are my friends.
shì. Tāmen shì wǒde péngyou.
是。他们是我的朋友。

3. No. They are not my friend.
bùshì. Tāmen bùshì wǒde péngyou.
不是。他们不是我的朋友。

Alternative Questions

Alternative questions, are formed by using 还是 (háishì) to join two possible answers for the replier to choose. For example:

1. Will you go to Beijing or Shanghai?
nǐ qù běijīng háishì qù shànghǎi?
你去北京还是去上海?

2. I will go to the Shanghai.
wǒ qù shànghǎi.
我去上海。

有 (*yǒu*) means to have and it indicates possession. 有 (*yǒu*) is negated when preceded by 没 (*méi*). For example:

1. How many books you have?
nǐ yǒu jí běn shū?
你有几本书?

2. I have three books.
wǒ yǒu sān běn shū.
我有三本书。

3. I don't have time.
wǒ méi yǒu shíjiān.
我没有时间。

Past Tense: The past tense of a verb in Chinese is made by adding the syllable 了 (*le*) immediately after the verb or at the very end of the sentence. For example:

1. They already left.
tāmen yǐjīng zǒu le.
她们已经走了。

2. I went to Shanghai.
wǒ qù le shànghǎi..
我去了上海。

However when there is 没有 *(méiyǒu)* in the sentence, 了 le is omitted. For example:

1. She has not eaten.
tā méiyǒu chī fàn.
她没有吃饭。

2. He has not gone out.
tā méiyǒu chū qu .
他没有出去。

Continuous Aspect

A verb followed immediately by the aspect particle¡ 着 (*zhe*) indicates the continuous aspect of an action or a state of affairs. For example:

1. We are watching movie.
wǒmen kàn zhe diànyǐng.
我们看着电影。

2. What are you listening?
nǐmen tīng zhe shénme?
你们听着什么？

Comparative Sentences

Type-1: The simplest form of comparative sentence would be as under **A** + 比 ***(bǐ)*** + **B** + **Appropriate adjective**. For example:

1. My book is better than his book.
wǒde shū bǐ tāde hǎo.
我的书比他的好。

Type-2: Comparisons of equality is generally expressed through , 跟。。。一样*(gēn...yíyàng)* construction, while inequality expressed through, 跟。。。不一样 *(gēn...bù yíyàng)*. For example:

1. My book is same as his book.
wǒde shū gēn tāde shū yíyàng.
我的书跟他的书一样。

2. My book is not same as his book.
wǒde shū gēn tāde shū bù yíyàng.
我的书跟他的书不一样。

Type-3: For comparisons of two different things or states, Chinese generally use 不如 *(bùrú)* construction. For example:

1. This shirt is not as good as that.
zhè jiàn chènyī bùrú nàjiàn hǎokàn.
这件衬衣不如那件好看。

Set Patterns and Constructions

1. The progressive aspect of an action.

To show the progressive aspect of an action, 正在。。。呢 *(zhèngzài...ne)* construction is used. For example:

A. Right now, I am studying.
wǒ zhèngzài xuéxí ne.
我正在学习呢。

2. 是。。。的 *(shì...de)* is an adverbial phrase of time, manner or place is emphasized by putting 是 *(shì)* in front and *(de)* after it. This construction can only be used where the action of the verb has been completed. For example:

A. That man has come from India.
nà ge rén shì cóng yìndù láide.
那个人是从印度来的。

3. 先。。。再。。。(x*ìan...zài)* shows a sequence of an action. For example:

A. First I will study and then play.
wǒ x*ìan xuéxí, zài wánr.*
我先学习，再玩儿。

4. 要。。。了 *(yào...le)* can be used to indicate that an action is going to take place very soon. Sometimes 就 *(jìu)* also can be added to intensify the action. For example:

A. Plane is about to fly.
fēijī jìu yào qǐfēi le.
飞机就要起飞了。

5. 一边。。。一边。。。*(yībīan...yībīan...)* is used when two action take place simultaneously. For example:

A. She reads while writing Chinese characters.
tā yībīan nìan, yībīan xiě hànzì.
她一边念，一边写汉字。

6. 有的。。。有的。。。*(yǒude... yǒude...)* means 'some...and others...'. For example:

A. Some people have come from India, and some from China.
yǒude rén shì cóng yìndù láide, yǒude rén shì cóng zhōngguó láide.
有的人是从印度来的，有的人是从中国来的。

7. 从。。。起 *(cóng...qǐ)* indicates an action from a particular time onwards. While, 从。。。到。。。 *(cóng...dào...)* means 'from…to…'. For example:

A. We have vacations from October onwards.
wǒmen cóng shí yuè qǐ fàngjià.
我们从十月起放假。

B. We have vacation from October to November.
wǒmen cóng shí yuè dào shíyī yuè fàngjià.
我们从十月到十一月放假。

8. 离。。。近/远 *(lí...jìn/yuǎn)* indicates the distance between the two places. If the distance is short we use 近 *(jìn)*, while if the distance is rather far it is 远 *(yuǎn)*. For example:

A. The Great Hall of the People is very near from the Imperial Palace.
Rénmín Dàhuìtáng lí Gùgōng hěn jìn.
人民大会堂离故宫很近。

B. My house is very far from here.
wǒ de jiā lí zhèr hěn yuǎn.
我的家离这儿很远。

9. 一。。。就。。。(*yī... jìu...*) indicates that two actions happen in close succession. The first clause states the circumstances and the second clause states the result. For example:

A. As soon as I reach China, I will write a letter to you.
wǒ yí dào zhōngguó jìu gěi nǐ xiěxìn.
我一到中国就给你写信。

10. 不但。。。而且。。。(*bùdàn... érqié...*) indicates a further development in meaning in the second clause from what started in the first one. (Not only…but…). For example:

A. She not only came late, but also not did her homework.
tā bùdàn lái de wǎn, érqié yě méi zuò tāde zuòyè.
她不但来得晚，而且也没作她的作业。

11. 虽然。。。但是。。。(*suīrán...dànshì...*) indicates 'although…but…' in English. For example:

A. Although he came late, but did his homework.
suīrán tā lái de wǎn, dànshì zuò le tāde zuòyè.
虽然他来得晚，但是作了他的作业。

12. 除了。。。以外。。。 *(chúle...yǐwài...)* mcans 'except' when used with 都 *(dōu)* but when used with 也 *(yě)* 还 *(hái)* or 又 *(yòu)*, it gives the meaning of 'besides' or 'in addition to'. For example:

A. Except him, all went to watch movie.
chúle tā yǐwài, měi ge rén dōu qù le kàn diànyǐng.
除了他以外，每个人 都去了看电影。

B. Apart from me, they can also speak Chinese.
chúle wǒ yǐwài, tāmen yě huì shuō hànyǔ.
除了我以外， 他们也会说汉语。

13. 越。。。越。。。*(yuè...yuè...)* indicates change in degree, while 越来越 *(yuè lái yuè)* indicating continuing change. For Example:

A. More I study Chinese more I find it interesting.
wǒ yuè xuéxí hànyǔ yuè juéde yǒuyìsi.
我越学习汉语越觉得有意思。

B. The level of our Chinese language is becoming better day by day.
wǒmen de hànyǔ shuǐpíng yuèlái yuè gāo.
我们的汉语水平越来越高。

Part-3

General Vocabulary

General Expressions	*Cháng yòng yǔ*	常用语
English	***pīnyīn***	**Chinese Characters**
Good morning	*zǎoshang hǎo*	早上好
Hello	*nǐ hǎo*	你好
Please	*qǐng*	请
Yes	*shì*	是
Good	*hǎo*	好
Very good	*hěn hǎo*	很好
Correct	*duì*	对
Ok	*xíng*	行
Thank you	*xiè xiè nín*	谢谢您

It's all right	*bíe kè qi*	别客气
Sorry	*duì bù qǐ*	对不起
Never mind	*méi guān xì*	没关系
Please excuse me	*qǐng yuán liàng*	请原谅
Please be seated	*qǐng zuò*	请座
Please come in	*qǐng jìn*	请进
Heartily thanks	*gǎn xiè*	感谢
Wait a moment	*děng yí xìa*	等一下
Good night	*wǎn ān*	晚安
See you again	*zài jiàn*	再见

Sentences:
jù zi:

句子：

Good morning everybody.
dà jiā zǎoshang hǎo
大家早上好。

Please help me.
qǐng bāng zhù wǒ.
请帮助我。

Sorry, I don't know.
duì bù qǐ, wǒ bú zhì dào.
对不起，我不知道。

Parts of the Body

Rénti

人体。

English	***pīnyīn***	**Chinese Characters**
Abdomen	*fù bù*	腹部
Ankle	*húai*	踝
Arm	*bì*	臂
Armpit	*yè wō*	腋窝
Back	*bèi*	背
Beard	*húxū*	胡须
Blood	*xuěyè*	血液
Bone	*gŭ gé*	骨骼
Brain	*dà năo*	大脑
Breast	*rŭfáng*	乳房

Cheek	*miàn jiá*	面颊
Chest	*xiōngbù*	胸部
Chin	*xiàbā*	下巴
Collarbone	*suógŭ*	锁骨
Ear	*ĕr*	耳
Elbow	*zhŏu*	肘
Eye	*yănjīng*	眼睛
Eyeball	*yănqíu*	眼球
Eyebrow	*méimáo*	眉毛
Face	*liăn*	脸
Finger	*shŏu zhĭ*	手指
Finger Nail	*zhĭ jia*	指甲
Index finger	*shí zhĭ*	食指
Middle finger	*zhōng zhĭ*	中指
Ring finger	*wúming zhĭ*	无名指

Little finger	*xiáo zhǐ*	小指
Foot	*jiǎo*	脚
Forehead	*é tóu*	额头
Hair	*tóufà*	头发
Hand	*shǒu*	手
Head	*tóu*	头
Heart	*xīn zàng*	心脏
Heel	*jiǎohòugēn*	脚后跟
Hip	*tún bù*	臀部
Knee	*xī gài*	膝盖
Kidney	*shèn*	肾
Leg	*tuǐ*	腿
Lip	*zuǐ chún*	嘴唇
Liver	*gān zàng*	肝脏
Lung	*fèi*	肺

Moustache	*zī*	髭
Mouth	*zuǐ*	嘴
Muscle	*jīròu*	肌肉
Neck	*jǐng*	颈
Nose	*bízí*	鼻子
Palm	*shǒu zhǎng*	手掌
Penis	*yīn jīng*	阴茎
Rib	*lēigǔ*	肋骨
Shoulder	*jiān*	肩
Skin	*pí fū*	皮肤
Stomach	*wèi*	胃
Thigh	*dà tuǐ*	大腿
Throat	*hóu*	嗓子
Thumb	*mú zhǐ*	拇指
Tongue	*shé tóu*	舌头

Tooth	*yáchi*	牙齿
Waist	*yāo*	要
Wrist	*wǎn*	腕

Sentences:

jù zi:

句子：

My throt is not well.
Wǒ de sǎng zi bù hǎo.
我的嗓子不好。

Her hairs are very good.
Tā de tóufà hěn hǎo.
她的头发很好。

I have a severe headache.
Wǒ tóu tòng de lìhai.
我头痛得厉害。

Household Articles

Jiāting wùpǐn
家庭物品

English	***pīnyīn***	**Chinese Characters**
Bathtub	*yù chí*	浴池
Bedding	*chuáng shàng yòngpǐn*	床上用品
Brush	*shuā zi*	刷子
Bucket	*tǒng*	桶
Candle	*là zhú*	蜡烛
Carpet	*dì tǎn*	地毯
Clock	*zhōng*	钟
Comb	*shū zi*	梳子
Cosmetic	*huà zhuāngpǐn*	化妆品

Curtain	*chuāng lián*	窗帘
Detergent	*xīyī fěn*	洗衣粉
Dinner sets	*cān jù*	餐具
Dinning table	*fàn zhuō*	饭桌
Dressing-table	*shū zhuāng tái*	梳妆台
Electric fan	*dìan shàn*	电扇
Electric iron	*dìan yùntǒu*	电熨斗
Fork	*chā zi*	叉子
Knife	*dāo zi*	刀子
Lamp	*tái dēng*	台灯
Lipstick	*chún gāo*	唇膏
Lock	*suǒ*	锁
Mirror	*jìng zi*	镜子
Mosquito net	*wén zhàng*	蚊帐
Needle	*zhēn*	针

Oven	*kăo xiāng*	烤箱
Pressure cooker	*gāo yà guō*	高压锅
Razor	*guā hú dāo*	刮胡刀
Refrigerator	*diàn bīngxiāng*	电冰箱
Sewing machine	*féng rèn jī*	缝纫机
Sink	*xí dí cáo*	洗涤槽
Soap	*féi zào*	肥皂
Sofa	*shā fā*	沙发
Spoon	*sháo zi*	勺子
Teapot	*chá hú*	茶壶
Tea-set	*chá jù*	茶具
Tea tray	*chá pán*	茶盘
Thread	*xiàn*	线
Toilet-roll	*shóu zhĭ*	手纸
Toothbrush	*yá shuā*	牙刷

Toothpaste	*yá gāo*	牙膏
Wardrobe	*yī guì*	衣柜
Washbasin	*guān xǐ chí*	盥洗池
Washing machine	*xǐ yījī*	洗衣机

Sentences:

jù zi:

句子：

Where are the candles?
là zhú zài nǎr?
蜡烛在哪？

I want to buy a refrigerator.
wǒ yào mǎi yī ge diàn bīngxiāng.
我要买一个电冰箱。

Please give me the toothpaste.
qíng nǐ gěi wǒ yá gāo.
请你给我牙膏。

Number & Quantities Cardinal Numbers

Shùzì hé shùliàng

数字 和 数量。

English	***pīnyīn***	**Chinese Characters**
0 zero	*líng*	零
1 one	*yī*	一
2 two	*èr*	二
3 three	*sān*	三
4 four	*sì*	四
5 five	*wǔ*	五
6 six	*lìu*	六
7 seven	*qī*	七
8 eight	*bā*	八
9 nine	*jiǔ*	九
10 ten	*shí*	十

11 eleven	*shí yī*	十一
12 twelve	*shí èr*	十二
13 thirteen	*shí sān*	十三
14 fourteen	*shí sì*	十四
15 fifteen	*shí wŭ*	十五
16 sixteen	*shí lìu*	十六
17 seventeen	*shí qī*	十七
18 eighteen	*shí bā*	十八
19 nineteen	*shí jiŭ*	十九
20 twenty	*èr shí*	二十
21 twenty one	*èr shí yī*	二十一
22 twenty two	*èr shí èr*	二十二
23 twenty three	*èr shí sān*	二十三
24 twenty four	*èr shí sì*	二十四
25 twenty five	*èr shí wŭ*	二十五
26 twenty six	*èr shí lìu*	二十六

27 twenty seven	*èr shí qī*	二十七
28 twenty eight	*èr shí bā*	二十八
29 twenty nine	*èr shí jiu*	二十九
30 thirty	*sān shí*	三十
31 thirty one	*sān shí yī*	三十一
32 thirty two	*sān shí èr*	三十二
33 thirty three	*sān shí sān*	三十三
34 thirty four	*sān shí sì*	三十四
35 thirty five	*sān shí wǔ*	三十五
36 thirty six	*sān shí lìu*	三十六
37 thirty seven	*sān shí qī*	三十七
38 thirty eight	*sān shí bā*	三十八
39 thirty nine	*sān shí jiǔ*	三十九
40 forty	*sì shí*	四十
41 forty one	*sì shí yī*	四十一
42 forty two	*sì shí èr*	四十二

43 forty three	*si shí sān*	四十三
44 forty four	*sì shí sì*	四十四
45 forty five	*s shí wǔ*	四十五
46 forty six	*sì shí lìu*	四十六
47 forty seven	*sì shí qī*	四十七
48 forty eight	*sì shí bā*	四十八
49 forty nine	*sì shí jiǔ*	四十九
50 fifty	*wǔshí*	五十
51 fifty one	*wǔshí yī*	五十一
52 fifty two	*wǔshí èr*	五十二
53 fifty three	*wǔshí sān*	五十三
54 fifty four	*wǔshí sì*	五十四
55 fifty five	*wǔshí wǔ*	五十五
56 fifty six	*wǔshí lìu*	五十六
57 fifty seven	*wǔ shí qī*	五十七
58 fifty eight	*wǔ shí bā*	五十八

59 fifty nine	*wŭshí jiŭ*	五十九
60 sixty	*lìu shí*	六十
61 sixty one	*lìu shí yī*	六十一
62 sixty two	*lìu shí èr*	六十二
63 sixty three	*lìu shí sān*	六十三
64 sixty four	*lìu shí sì*	六十四
65 sixty five	*lìu shí wŭ*	六十五
66 sixty six	*lìu shí lìu*	六十六
67 sixty seven	*lìu shí qī*	六十七
68 sixty eight	*lìu shí bā*	六十八
69 sixty nine	*lìu shí jiŭ*	六十九
70 seventy	*qī shí*	七十
71 seventy one	*qī shí yī*	七十一
72 seventy two	*qī shí èr*	七十二
73 seventy three	*qī shí sān*	七十三

74 seventy four	*qī shí sì*	七十四
75 seventy five	*qī shí wǔ*	七十五
76 seventy six	*qī shí lìu*	七十六
77 seventy seven	*qī shí qī*	七十七
78 seventy eight	*qī shí bā*	七十八
79 seventy nine	*qī shí jiǔ*	七十九
80 eighty	*bā shí*	八十
81 eighty one	*bā shí yī*	八十一
82 eighty two	*bā shí èr*	八十二
83 eighty three	*bā shí sān*	八十三
84 eighty four	*bā shí sì*	八十四
85 eighty five	*bā shí wǔ*	八十五
86 eighty six	*bā shí lìu*	八十六
87 eighty seven	*bā shí qī*	八十七
88 eighty eight	*bā shí bā*	八十八

89 eighty nine	*bā shí jiŭ*	八十九
90 ninety	*jiŭ shí*	九十
91 ninety one	*jiŭ shí yī*	九十一
92 ninety two	*jiŭ shí èr*	九十二
93 ninety three	*jiŭ shí sān*	九十三
94 ninety four	*jiŭ shí sì*	九十四
95 ninety five	*jiŭ shí wŭ*	九十五
96 ninety six	*jiŭ shí lìu*	九十六
97 ninety seven	*jiŭ shí qī*	九十七
98 ninety eight	*jiŭ shí bā*	九十八
99 ninety nine	*jiŭ shí jiŭ*	九十九
100 Hundred	*yī băi*	一百
101 one hundred one	*yī băi líng yī*	一百零一
102 one hundred two	*yī băi líng èr*	一百零二
103 one hundred three	*yī băi líng sān*	一百零三

104 one hundred four	*yī bǎi líng sì*	一百零四
105 one hundred five	*yī bǎi líng wǔ*	一百零五
106 one hundred six	*yī bǎi líng lìu*	一百零六
107 one hundred sevenv	*yī bǎi líng qī*	一百零七
108 one hundred eight	*yī bǎi líng bā*	一百零八
109 one hundred nine	*yī bǎi líng jiǔ*	一百零九
110 one hundred ten	*yī bǎi yī shí*	一百一十
111 one hundred eleven	*yī bǎi yī shí yī*	一百一十一
112 one hundred twelve	*yī bǎi yī shí èr*	一百一十二
113 one hundred thirteen	*yī bǎi yī shí sān*	一百一十三
114 one hundred fourteen	*yī bǎi yī shí sì*	一百一十四
115 one hundred fifteen	*yī bǎi yī shí wǔ*	一百一十五
116 one hundred sixteen	*yī bǎi yī shí lìu*	一百一十六
117 one hundred seventeen	*yī bǎi yī shí qī*	一百一十七
118 one hundred eighteen	*yī bǎi yī shí bā*	一百一十八
119 one hundred nineteen	*yī bǎi yī shí jiǔ*	一百一十九

120 one hundred twenty	*yī bǎi èr shí*	一百二十
200 Two Hundred	*èr bǎi*	二百
300 Three Hundred	*sān bǎi*	三百
400 Four Hundred	*sì bǎi*	四百
500 Five Hundred	*wǔbǎi*	五百
600 Six Hundred	*lìu bǎi*	六百
700 Seven Hundred	*qī bǎi*	七百
800 Eight Hundred	*bā bǎi*	八百
900 Nine Hundred	*jiǔ bǎi*	九百
1000 One Thousand	*yī qiān*	一千
10,000 Ten thousand	*yī wàn*	一万
100,000 Hundred thousand (One Lac)	*shí wàn*	十万
1,000,000 One million	*bǎi wàn*	百万
100,000,00 Ten million (one Crore)	*qiān wàn*	千万

100,000,000 Hundred million	*yīyì*	一亿
1,000,000,000 One billion	*shí yì*	十亿

Sentences:

jù zi:

句子：

I have Eight hundred American dollars.
wǒ yǒu bā bǎi měi yuán.
我有八百美元。

This mobile is of Ten thousand rupees.
zhè ge shǒu jī de jiágè shì yī wàn lú bǐ.
这个手机的价格是一万卢比.

The population of India is more than One billion.
yìn dù de rénkǒu shì shí yī duǒ.
印度的人口是十亿多

Ordinal Number

xù shù

序数

English	***pīnyīn***	**Chinese Characters**
First	*dì yī*	第一
Second	*dì èr*	第二
Third	*dì sān*	第三
First one	*dì yī gè*	第一个
Second one	*dì èr gè*	第二个
Third one	*dì sān gè*	第三个
First time	*dì yī cì*	第一次
Second time	*dì èr cì*	第二次
Third time	*dì sān cì*	第三次

entences:

ù zi:

句子：

'lease open first chapter.

íng nǐmen dǎkāi dì yī kè.

青你们打开第一课。

econd one is my manager.

ì èr gè rén shì wǒ de jīnglǐ.

第二个人是我的经理。

'his is the third time I came to China.

hè shì dì sān cì wǒ dào zhōng guó lái.

这是第三次我到中国来。

Percentages

Băi fēnshù

百分数

English Characters	***pīnyīn***	**Chinese**
5%	*băi fēnzhī wŭ*	百分之五
12.5%	*băi fēnzhī shí èr diăn wŭ*	百分之十二点五
25%	*băi fēnzhī èr shí wŭ*	百分之二十五
50%	*băi fēnzhī wŭ shí*	百分之五十
75%	*băi fēnzhī qī shí wŭ*	百分之七十五
100%	*băi fēnzhī băi*	百分之百

Fractions

ēnshù

‑数

nglish	*pīnyīn*	Chinese Characters
2	*ér fēnzhī yī*	二分之一
4	*sì fēnzhī yī*	四分之一
3	*sān fēnzhī ér*	三分之二
4	*sì fēnzhī sān*	四分之三

ntences:

zi:

子：

s 100% cotton.

è jìu shì bǎi fēnzhī bǎi de miánhua.

就是百分之百的棉花。

Our class has ¾ girl students.
Wǒmen bān sì fēnzhī sān shì nǚ xuésheng.
我们班四分之三是女学生。

There is 10% discount on these items.
zhè xiē dōngxī da zhé kòu bǎi fēnzhī jiǔ shí.
这些东西打折扣百分之九十。

Days, Months and Season

Xīngqī, yuè hé jìjié

星期 月 和 季节

English	***pīnyīn***	**Chinese Characters**
	Days ***Xīngqī*** 星期	
Monday	*Xīngqī yī*	星期一
Tuesday	*Xīngqī èr*	星期二
Wednesday	*Xīngqī sān*	星期三
Thursday	*Xīngqī sì*	星期四
Friday	*Xīngqī wŭ*	星期五
Saturday	*Xīngqī lìu*	星期六
Sunday	*Xīngqī rì* also *Xīngqī tiān*	星期日 / 星期 天

Sentences:

jù zi:

句子：

Today is Friday.
jīn tiān shì xīngqī wǔ
今天是星期五。

Months
Yuèfen
月份

January	*yī yuè*	一月
February	*èr yuè*	二月
March	*sān yuè*	三月
April	*sì yuè*	四月
May	*wǔ yuè*	五月
June	*lìu yuè*	六月

July	*qí yuè*	七月
August	*bā yuè*	八月
September	*jiǔ yuè*	九月
October	*shí yuè*	十月
November	*shí yī yuè*	十一月
December	*shí ér yuè*	十二月

Sentences:

jù zi:

句子：

Next month is March.
xià yuè shì sān yuè or xià ge yuè shì sān yuè
下月是三月。or 下个月是三月。

Next month is........
xià yuè shì... or xià ge yuè shì ....
下月是...... or 下个月是......

Season
Jìjié
季节

Spring	*chūn tiān*	春天
Summer	*xià tiān*	夏天
Autumn	*qiū tiān*	秋天
Rainy season	*yǔ jì*	雨季
Winter	*dōng tiān*	冬天

Sentences:

jù zi:

句子：

Now it is autumn season.
Xiàn zài shì qiū tiān le.
现在是秋天了。

***Timc scquence goes like this in Chinese:**

Year/Month/Day/Week/Time.
Nián/yuè/tiān/xīngqī/shí jiān.
年 / 月 / 天 / 星期 / 时间。

If it is *Thursday 12th October 2006* in English, it will like this in Chinese:
Èr línglíng lìu nián, shí yuè, shí èrhào, xīngqī sì.
二零零六年(2006)，十月(Oct.), 十二号(12th),

星期四(Thursday).

Today is 7th May 2007.
jīn tiān shì èr líng líng qī nián, wǔ yuè, qī hào.
今天是二零零七年五月七号。

Chinese Currency

Zhōng guó huò bì

中国货币

English	***pīnyīn***	**Chinese Characters**	
The people's currency (RMB)			
	rén mín bì	人民币	
A unit of Chinese money.			
	yuán (kuài)*	元	(块)
A unit of Chinese money.			
	jiǎo (máo)*	角	(毛)
A unit of Chinese money.			
	fēn	分	

1元 *yuán* =10 角 */10* 毛 *máo*

1角 *jiăo* =10 分 *fēn*

* In colloquial speech, *yuán* is sometimes called as *kuài*, and *jiăo* is called *máo*, while *fēn* is often dropped. For example if it is 1.35 RMB. It will be said like:

yī kuài sān máo wu.

一块三毛五。

Clothes and Garments

Yīliào jí fúzhuāng
衣料 及 服装

English	*pīnyīn*	Chinese Characters
Apron	*wéi qún*	围裙
Bed sheet	*chuáng dān*	床单
Belt	*pí dài*	皮带
Blanket	*tǎnzi*	毯子
Blouse	*nǚ shì chénshān*	女式衬衫
Bow	*lǐngjié*	领结
Button	*niǔ kòu*	纽扣
Canvas	*fán bù*	帆布
Coat	*shàng yī*	上衣
Cushion	*yǐ diǎn*	椅垫

Gloves	*shǒu tào*	手套
Gown	*cháng wài yī*	长外衣
Hat	*màozi*	帽子
Handkerchief	*shǒu pà*	手帕
Jacket	*jiá kè shān*	夹克衫
Leather shoes	*pí xié*	皮鞋
Muffler	*wéi jīn*	围巾
Napkin	*cān jīn*	餐巾
Overcoat	*dà yī*	大衣
Pocket	*kǒu dài*	口袋
Quilt	*mián bèi*	棉被
Raincoat	*yǔ yī*	雨衣
Scarf	*tóu jīn*	头巾
Shirt	*chènshān*	衬衫

Shorts	*duǎnkù*	短裤
Skirt	*qúnzi*	裙子
Sleeve	*xìuzi*	袖子
Stocking	*cháng wà*	长袜
Sportswear	*yùndòng fú*	运动服
Sweater	*máo yī*	毛衣
Suit	*xī zhuāng*	西装
T-Shirt	*hàn shān*	汗衫
Towel	*máo jīn*	毛巾
Trousers	*kùzi*	裤子
Tie	*lǐng dài*	领带
Underwear	*nèi yi*	内衣
Waistcoat	*bèi xīn*	背心
Wedding gown	*hūn shā*	婚纱

Sentences:

jù zi:

句子：

This bed sheet is very good.
zhè zhāng chuáng dān hěn hăo kàn.
这张床单很好看。

That pair of trousers is for how much?
nà shuāng kùzi duōshao qián?
那双裤子多少钱？

I want red colour shirt.
wŏ yào hóng sè de chènshān.
我要红色的衬衫。

I want....... colour shirt.
wŏ yào .... sè de chènshān.
我要........的衬衫。

Sports

Tǐyù

体育

English	*pīnyīn*	Chinese Characters
Badminton	*yǔ máo qíu*	羽毛球
Baseball	*bàng qíu*	棒球
Basketball	*lán qíu*	篮球
Billiards	*tái qíu*	台球
Boxing	*quán jī*	拳击
Cricket	*bǎn qíu*	板球
Ice-skating	*huá bīng*	滑冰
Football	*zú qíu*	足球
Golf	*gāo ěr fū qíu*	高尔夫球

Gymnastics	*tǐ cāo*	体操
Handball	*shǒu qíu*	手球
High jump	*tiào gāo*	跳高
Hockey	*qū gùn qíu*	曲棍球
Javelin throw	*biāo qiāng*	标枪
Long jump	*tiào yuǎn*	跳远
Marathon	*mǎ lā sōng*	马拉松
Martial arts	*wǔ shù*	武术
Polo	*má qiú*	马球
Shooting	*shè jī*	射击
Skiing	*huá shǔi*	滑水
Sprint	*duǎn pǎo*	短跑
Swimming	*yóu yǒng*	游泳
Table tennis	*pīng pāng qíu*	乒乓球

Tennis	*wăng qíu*	网球
Volleyball	*pái qíu*	排球
Water polo	*shŭi qiú*	水球
Wrestling	*shuāi jīao*	摔跤
Asian Games	*yà yùn huì*	亚运会
Lose	*shū*	输
Match	*bĭsài*	比赛
Olympics	*ào yùn huì*	奥运会
Referee	*cái pàn*	裁判
Team	*duì*	队
Win	*yíng*	赢

Sentences:

jù zi:

句子：

I like playing badminton.
wǒ xǐ huan dǎ yǔ máo qíu.
我喜欢打羽毛球。

Do you like playing volleyball?
nǐ xǐ huan bù xǐhuan dǎ pái qíu?
你喜欢不喜欢打排球？

This time Olympics will be held in Beijing.
zhè cì ào yùn huì zài běijīng jǔ xíng.
这次奥运会在北京举行。

Colors

Yán sè

颜色

English	***pīnyīn***	**Chinese Characters**
Ash/gray	*huī sè*	灰色
Black	*hēi sè*	黑色
Blue	*lán sè*	蓝色
Blue gray	*lán huī sè*	蓝灰色
Brown	*zōng sè*	棕色
Golden	*jīn sè*	金色
Green	*lǜ sè*	绿色
Orange	*jú hóng sè*	橘红色
Pink	*fěn hóng sè*	粉红色
Purple	*zǐ sè*	紫色
Red	*hóng sè*	红色

Saffron	*jú huáng sè*	橘黄色
Silver	*yín sè*	银色
Violet	*zǐ luó lán sè*	紫罗兰色
White	*bái sè*	白色
Yellow	*huáng sè*	黄色

Sentences:

jù zi:

句子：

I like red colour.
wǒ xǐ huan hóng yán sè.
我喜欢红颜色。

This is a white shirt.
zhè shì yī jiàn bái sè de chènshān.
这是一件白颜色的衬衫。

My sweater is of green colour.
wo de máoyī shì lǜ sè de.
我的毛衣是绿色的。

Animals

Dòng wù

动物

English	*pīnyīn*	Chinese Characters
Alligator	*měi zhōu è yǔ*	美洲鳄鱼
Ant	*má yǐ*	蚂蚁
Bear	*xióng*	熊
Buffalo	*shuǐ níu*	水牛
Bull	*gōng níu*	公牛
Camel	*luò tuo*	骆驼
Cat	*māo*	猫
Cattle	*níu*	牛
Crocodile	*è yǔ*	鳄鱼
Cow	*mǔ níu*	母牛

Deer	*lù*	鹿
Dog	*gǒu*	狗
Dolphin	*hǎi tún*	海豚
Donkey	*lǘ*	驴
Dragon	*lóng*	龙
Elephant	*dà xiàng*	大象
Earthworm	*qīu yin*	蚯蚓
Fox	*hú li*	狐狸
Frog	*qīngwā*	青蛙
Goat	*shān yáng*	山羊
Horse	*mǎ*	马
Hippopotamus	*hé mǎ*	河马
Jackal	*hú láng*	狐狼
Kangaroo	*dài shǔ*	袋鼠
Lion	*shīzi*	狮子

Leopard	*měi zhōu bào*	美洲豹
Lizard	*xī yì*	蜥蜴
Mongoose	*māo yòu*	貌鼬
Mule	*luó*	骡
Monkey	*hóuzi*	猴子
Panda	*xióng māo*	熊猫
Panther	*bào*	豹
Pig	*zhū*	猪
Rat	*dà shŭ*	大鼠
Rabbit	*tù zi*	兔子
Rhinoceros	*xī níu*	犀牛
Scorpion	*xiē zi*	蝎子
Seal	*hăi bào*	海豹
Shark	*shā yú*	鲨鱼
Snake	*shé*	蛇

Sheep	*yáng*	羊
Spider	*zhī zhū*	蜘蛛
Tiger	*láo hŭ*	老虎
Turtle	*hăi guī*	海龟
Zebra	*bān má*	斑马

Sentences:

jù zi:

句子：

Tiger is the National animal of India.
láo hŭ shì yìn dù de guó wù.
老虎是印度的国物。

Panda is the National animal of China.
xióng māo shì zhōng guó de guó wù.
熊猫是中国的国物。

I like horse riding.
wŏ xĭ huan qí mă.
我喜欢骑马。

Birds

Niăo

鸟

English	***pīnyīn***	**Chinese Characters**
Butterfly	*hú dié*	蝴蝶
Crane	*hè*	鹤
Crow	*wū yā*	乌鸦
Cuckoo	*bù gú niăo*	布谷鸟
Dragonfly	*qīng ting*	蜻蜓
Dove	*gē zi*	鸽子
Duck	*yā zi*	鸭子
Eagle	*yīng*	鹰
Fly	*cāng yīng*	苍蝇

Grasshopper	*zhà měng*	蚱蜢
Hen	*mŭ jī*	母鸡
Mosquito	*wén zi*	蚊子
Owl	*māo tóu yīng*	猫头鹰
Peacock	*kŏng què*	孔雀
Penguin	*qi'é*	企鹅
Parrot	*yīng wū*	鹦鹉
Pigeon	*gē zi*	鸽子
Sparrow	*má què*	麻雀
Woodpecker	*zhuó mù niăo*	啄木鸟

Sentences:

jù zi:

句子：

Peacock is the National bird of India.
kǒng què shì yìn dù de guó niǎo.
孔雀是印度的国鸟。

These ducks are very beautiful.
Zhè xiē yā zi hěn piàoliang.
这些鸭子很漂亮。

Here are so many crows.
Zhè li yóu hěn duō wū yā.
这里有很多乌鸦。

Fruits

Shuǐ Guǒ

水果

English	*pīnyīn*	Chinese Characters
Almond	*xìng rén*	杏仁
Apple	*píng guǒ*	苹果
Apricot	*xìng zi*	杏子
Banana	*xiāng jiāo*	香蕉
Cashew nut	*yāo guǒ*	腰果
Cheery	*yīng táo*	樱桃
Coconut	*yē zi*	椰子
Date	*zǎo yē zi*	枣椰子
Grapes	*pú táo*	葡萄
Leeches	*lì zhī*	荔枝

Mango	*máng guǒ*	芒果
Orange	*jú zi*	橘子
Papaya	*mù guā*	木瓜
Pomegranate	*shī līu*	石榴
Pineapple	*bō luó*	菠萝
Peach	*táo zi*	桃子
Pear	*lí zi*	梨子
Strawberry	*cǎo méi*	草莓
Sugarcane	*gān zhè*	甘蔗
Walnut	*hú táo*	胡桃
Watermelon	*xī guā*	西瓜

Sentences:

jù zi:

句子：

I want some apples.
wǒ yào yī xiē píng guǒ.
我要一些苹果。

I like eating mangoes very much.
wǒ hén xǐ huan chī máng guǒ.
我很喜欢吃芒果。

Do you have pomegranates?
Ní yǒu shī līu ma?
你有石榴吗？

I like.......
wǒ xǐ huan......
我喜欢.......

Vegetables

shū cài

蔬菜

English	***pīnyīn***	**Chinese Characters**
Bamboo shoots	*sǔn zi*	笋子
Beans	*dòu zi*	豆子
Beetroot	*hóng cài tóu*	红彩头
Brinjal	*qié zi*	茄子
Cabbage	*yuán bǎi cài*	元白菜
Carrot	*hú luó bù*	胡萝卜
Cucumber	*huáng guā*	黄瓜
Cauliflower	*cài huā*	菜花
Chinese cabbage	*dà bǎi cài*	大白菜
Ginger	*jiàng*	姜

Garlic	*dà suàn*	大蒜
Leamon	*níng méng*	柠檬
Mushroom	*mó gū*	蘑菇
Onion	*yáng cōng*	洋葱
Peas	*wān dòu*	碗豆
Potato	*tǔ dòu*	土豆
Radish	*xiáo luó bù*	小萝卜
Spinch	*bō cài*	菠菜
Tomato	*xī hóng shì / fānqié*	西红柿 / 番茄

Sentences:

jù zi:

句子：

I want some potato.
wǒ yào yī xiě tǔ dòu.
我要一些土豆。

Do you eat cucumber?
nǐ chī bù chī huáng guā?
你吃不吃黄瓜？

I eat carrots everyday.
wǒ měi tiān chī hú luó bù.
我每天吃胡萝卜。

I want........
wǒ yaò........
我要。。。。

Transport and Communication

Jiāo tōng yùn shū

交通运输

English	***pīnyīn***	**Chinese Characters**
Aeroplane	*fēi jī*	飞机
Boat	*xiǎo chuán*	小船
Bulldozer	*tuī tǔ jī*	推土机
Bus	*gōng gòng qì chē*	公共汽车
Car	*qì chē*	汽车
Crane	*qǐ zhòng jī*	起重机
Cycle	*zì xíng chē*	自行车
Glider	*huá xiáng jī*	滑翔机
Helicopter	*zhí shēng jī*	直升机

Horse cart	*mă chē*	马车
Jeep	*jí pŭ chē*	吉普车
Motorboat	*mó tuō ting*	摩托艇
Motorcycle	*mó tuō chē*	摩托车
Parachute	*jiàng luò săn*	降落伞
Rickshaw	*rén lì sān lún chē*	人力三轮车
Ship	*chuán*	船
Three-wheeler	*sān lún chē*	三轮车
Train	*huŏ chē*	火车
Tram	*yŏu guĭ diàn chē*	有轨电车
Truck	*dà chē*	火车
Van	*miàn bāo chē*	面包车。

Sentences:

jù zi:

句子：

I came by aeroplane.

wǒ shì zuò fēi jī lái de.

我是坐飞机来的。

I like riding bicycle.

wǒ xǐ huan qí zì xíng chē.

我喜欢骑自行车.

We will go by train.

wǒmen zuò huǒ chē qù.

我们坐火车去。

Family Relations

Qīn shu / qīn qì

亲属 / 亲戚

English	*pīnyīn*	Chinese Characters
Father	*fù qīn*	父亲
Mother	*mŭ qīn*	母亲
Grand Father (paternal)	*zŭ fù*	祖父
Grand Mother (paternal)	*zŭ mŭ*	祖母
Grand Father (maternal)	*wài zŭ fù*	外祖父
Grand Mother (maternal)	*wài zŭ mŭ*	外祖母
Husband	*zhàng fu*	丈夫

Wife	*qī zi*	妻了
Son	*ér zi*	儿子
Daughter-in-law	*ér xí*	儿媳
Daughter	*nŭ ér*	女儿
Son-in-law	*nŭ xu*	女婿
Elder Brother	*gē ge*	哥哥
(His wife)	*săo sao*	嫂嫂
Yonger Brother	*dì dì*	弟弟
(His wife)	*dì mèi*	弟妹
Elder Sister	*jiĕ jie*	姐姐
(Her husband)	*jiĕ fu*	姐夫
Younger Sister	*mèi mei*	妹妹
(Her husband)	*mèi fu*	妹夫
Father's Elder Brother	*bó bo*	伯伯

(His wife)	*bó mā*	伯妈
Father's Yonger Brother	*shū shu*	叔叔
(His wife)	*shū shen*	婶婶
Father's Sister	*gū gu*	姑姑
(Her husband)	*gū fu*	姑父
Mother's Sister	*yí*	姨
(Her husband)	*yí fù*	姨父
Mother's Brother	*jìu jiu*	舅舅
(His wife)	*jìu mā*	舅妈
Cousin Brother	*biǎo xiōng*	表兄
Cousin Sister	*biǎo jiě*	表姐
Step-father	*jì fù*	继父
Step-mother	*jì mǔ*	继母

Sentences:

jù zi:

句子：

He is my father.

tā shì wǒ de fù qīn.

他是我的父亲。

She is my younger sister.

tā shì wǒ de mèi mei.

他是我的妹妹。

My mother is doctor.

wǒ de mǔ qīn shì yī shēng.

我的母亲是医生。

Directions

fāng xiàng

方向

English	***pīnyīn***	**Chinese Characters**
East	*dōng biān*	东边
West	*xī biān*	西边
North	*běi biān*	北边
South	*nán biān*	南边
Inside	*lǐ biān*	里边
Outside	*wài biān*	外边
Frontside	*qián biān*	前边
Backside	*hòu biān*	后边
Top, above, over	*shàng biān*	上边
Bottom, below	*xià biān*	下边
Middle, center, between	*zhōng jiān*	中间

Sentcnces:

jù zi:

句子:

I am standing on the eastern side.
wǒ zhàn zài dōng biān.
我站在东边。

It is very cold outside.
wài biān hén lěng.
外边很冷。

My hotel is at the north side of the city.
wǒ de bīn guǎn zài chéng shì de běi biān.
我的宾馆在城市的北边。

Part-4

Conversational Chinese

Introducing Oneself

自我介绍。

Dialogues:
huì huà:
会话:

A: What is your surname?
Nǐn guì xìng?
您贵姓?

B: My surname is Liu.
Wǒ xìng líu.
我姓刘。

A: What is your name?
Nǐ jiào shénme míngzi?
你叫什么名字?

B: My name is Kumar.
Wǒ jiào kǔ mǎ ěr.
我叫苦吗尔。

A: How old are you?
Nǐ duōdà le?
你多大了？

B: I am 35.
Wǒ sān shí wǔ suì le.
我三十五岁了。

A: Are you married?
Nǐ jiéhūn le ma?
你结婚了吗？

B: I am married.
Wǒ jiéhūn le.
我结婚了。

A: How many children do you have?
Nǐ yǒu jǐ gè háizi?
你有几个孩子？

B: I have two children. One is boy and one is girl.
Wǒ yǒu liǎng gè. Yī gè shì nán hái, Yī gè shì nǚ hái.
我有两个。一个是男孩，一个是女孩。

A: Does your wife work?
Nǐ de tài tài gōng zuò ma?
你的太太工作吗？

B: Yes, My wife works. She is a teacher.
Duì, wǒ de tài tài gōng zuò. tā shì lǎo shī.
对，我的太太工作。她是老师。

A: Where do you live?
Nǐ zhù zài nǎer?
你住在哪儿？

B: I live in New Delhi.
Wǒ zhù zài xīn déli.
我住在新德里。

Jiè shào biéren

介绍别人

Introducing People

Dialogues:
huì huà:
会话：

A: Aimei, this is Mr. Kumar, and this is Mrs. Kumar. They have just come from India.
Àiméi, zhè wèi shì kŭ mă ĕr xiān sheng, tā shì tā de tài tài. Tāmen gāng cóng yìn dù lái.
爱梅， 这位是苦吗尔先生，她是他的太太。
他们刚从印度来。

B: How are you?
Nĭmen hăo?
你们好？

A: Fine, thanks. She is my wife Aimei.
Hĕn hăo, xiè xiè. tā shì Àiméi, wŏde tài tài.
很好，谢谢。她是爱梅，我的太太。

B: We are very much interested in meeting Chinese family

Wŏmen hĕn xĭhuan kàn kàn zhōngguó de jiātíng.

我们很喜欢看看中国的家庭。

A: Oh, welcome!

Ò, huān yíng, huān yíng.

哦，欢迎，欢迎。

B: How many members you have in your family?

Nĭ jiā yŏu jĭ kŏu rén?

你家有几口 人？

A: We have four members in our family.

Wŏmen jiā yŏu sì gè rén.

我们家有四个人。

B: She is my daughter, Wang Lili.

Tā shì wŏ de nŭer, Wáng Lìli. Tā shì zhōng xuéshen

她是我的女儿王丽丽。

B: She is a high school student.
Tā shì zhōng xuésheng.
她是中学生。

B: He is my son.
Tā shì wǒ de èr zi.
他是我的儿子。

B: My son is studying at the university.
Wǒ de érzi zài dàxué lǐ xuéxi.
我的儿子在大学里学习

B: Please sit down and have some tea.
Dà jiā qǐng zuò a, qǐng hē chá ba.
大家请座啊，请喝茶吧。

zài jī chăng

在机场

At the Airport

Dialogues:

huì huà:

会话：

A: Hello! Are you Mr. Kumar from India?
nín hăo! nín shì yìn dù lái de kŭ mă ĕr xiān sheng ma?
您好！您是印度来的苦马尔先生吗？

B: Yes! I' am Mr. Kumar from India.
shì! wŏ shì cóng yìn dù lái de kŭ mă ĕr xiān sheng.
是！ 我是从印度来的苦吗尔先生。

B: May I ask your name?
nín guì xìng?
您贵姓？

A: I am Li. I specially came from Beijing Hotel to receive you.
wǒ xìng lǐ. wǒ shì cóng běi jīng fàn diàn tè yì lái jiē nín de.
我姓李。我是从北京饭店特意来接您的。

B: Thank you for specialy coming & recieving me.
xiè xiè nín tè yì lái jiē wǒ.
谢谢您特意来接我。

B: I am very glad to meet you.
rèn shi ní wǒ hěn gāo xìng.
认识你我很高兴。

A: How was your journey?
nín yí lù shang hǎo ma?
您一路上好吗？

B: I had a very smooth journey.
wǒ yí lù shang hěn hǎo.
我一路上很好。

A: Is this the first time you have come to China?
nín shì dì yī cè lái zhōng guó ma?
您是第一次来中国吗？

B: Yes, it is the first time.
shì, dì yī cè lái.
是，第一次来。

B： I am really very happy.
wǒ fēi cháng gāo xìng.
我非常高兴。

B： During my stay in China kindly assist me as good as you can.
Zài zhōng guó qī jiān, qǐng nǐ men duō duō guān zhào wǒ.
在中国期间，请你们多多关照我。

A: Please don't be so polite.
bú yòng kè qi.
不用客气。

A: We are very glad welcoming you.
wǒ men fēi cháng huān yíng nín.
我们非常欢迎您。

A: Has your entire luggage arrived?
nín de xíngli dōu dào le ma?
您的行李都到了吗？

B: I haven't found it yet.
wǒ hái méi zhǎo dào.
我还没找到。

A: Please give me your luggage claim slip. I will help you finding it.
nín gěi wǒ nín de xíngli dān. bāng nín zhǎo yì zhǎo.
请您给我 您的行李单。帮您找一找。

B: Thank you.
xiè xiè!
谢谢！

zài hăi guān

在海关

At the Customs

Dialogues:

huì huà:

会话：

A: Hello! Welcome to China.
nín hăo! huān yíng nín dào zhōng guó lái.
您好！欢迎您到中国来。

A: Let me have a look to your passport and visa.
qĭng ràng wŏ kàn yí xià nín de hù zhào hé qiān zhèng.
请让我看一下您的护照和签证。

B: This is my passport and visa.
zhè shì wŏ de hù zhào hé qiān zhèng.
这是我的护照和签证。

A: How much luggage do you have?
nín yŏu jĭ jiàn xíngli?
您有几件行李？

B: Just have two traveling bags.
zhí yǒu liǎng jiàn lǚ xíng bāo.
只有两件旅行包。

A: Ok. What do the travel bags contain?
hǎo ba. lǐbian yǒu shénma dōngxi?
好吧。里边有什么东西？

B: Have some clothes and personal belongings.
yǒu yì xiě yīfu hé zì yòng wù pin.
有一些衣服和自用物品。

A: Is there anything to be declared?
yǒu méi yǒu shénma shēn bào de dōngxi?
有没有什么申报的东西？

B: I don't know. Please tell me which things need to be declared?
Bù zhī daò. qǐng gào sǔ wǒ nǎ xiē dōngxi yào shēn bào?
不知道。请告诉我哪些东西要申报？

A: The back of the luggage declaration form has a list of items that needs to be declared.
xíngli shēn bào dān de bèi biàn xiě le xū yào dōngxi de míng chēng.
行李申报单的背面写了需要东西的名称。

A: Please take a look at it.
qǐng kàn yí xià.
请看一下。

B: I don't have such things to be declared.
wǒ méi yǒu yào shēn bào de dōngxi.
我没有要申报的东西。

B: Where is the money exchange counter?
wài huì duì huàn chù zài nǎr?
外汇兑换处 在哪儿？

A: Money exchange counter is very close from here.
wài huì duì huàn chù lí zhèr hěn jìn.
外汇兑换处离这儿很近。

A: Go towards right, after hundred meters you will be there.
wăng yòu zŏu, yī bài mĭ jìu dào le.
往右走，一百米就到了。

B: Thank you.
xiè xiè.
谢谢。

zài bīn guǎn

在宾馆

At the Hotel

Dialogues:

huì huà:

会话：

A： Miss. I am Mr. Kumar from India.
Xiǎo jie, wǒ shì cóng yìn dù lái de kǔ mǎ ěr xiān sheng.
小姐，我是从印度来的苦马尔 先生.。

A： I had booked Room no. 212.
wǒ yù dìng le èr yāo èr fáng jiān.
我预订了 212 房间。

B： Welcome to our hotel. Please come with me.
Huānyíng guāng lín. qǐng gēn wǒ lái.
欢迎光临。请跟我来。

B： This is your room. What do you think of it?
zhè jìu shì nín de fáng jiān. nín jué de zěnmeyàng?
这就是您的房间。您觉得怎么样？

A： This room is very good.
Zhè gè fáng jiān hěn hǎo.
这个房间很好。

A: But does not have a balcony, I would like a room with balcony.
dān shì méi yǒu yáng tái, wǒ yào yī gè yǒu yáng tái de fáng jiān.
但是没有阳台，我要一个有阳台的房间。

B： No problem, we can provide you a room with balcony¡
méi yǒu wèn tí, wǒmen kě yí gěi nín yī gè yǒu yáng tái de fáng jiān.
没有问题，我们可以给您一个有阳台的房间。

A： What is the rent per day for that room?
nà gè fáng jiān yì tiān duō shǎo qián?
那个房间一天多少钱？

B： Hundred U.S. Dollar per day.
yì bǎi měi yuán.
一百美元。

A： Excuse me; can I make the long distance calls? (I.S.D.)
qǐng wèn, wǒ néng bù néng dǎ guó jì cháng tú diàn huà?
请问，我能不能打国际长途电话？

B： Every room is having a Telephone. From there you can contact to Telephone operator.
měi gè fáng jiān yǒu diàn huà. nín kě yí tōng guò huà wù yuán dǎ.
每个房间有电话。您可以通过话务员打。

A： Is hotel having Internet Center?
bīn guǎn yǒu méi yǒu yīn tè wǎng zhōng xīn?
宾馆有没有因特网中心？

B： We have. At the commercial center on the first floor.
yǒu. zài yī céng shāng wù zhōng xīn.
有。在一层商务中心。

A： Excuse me; where is the restaurant?
qǐng wèn, cān tīng zài shénma dì fang?
请问，餐厅在什么地方？

B： Restaurant is on the right side of commercial center on the first floor.
cān tīng zài yī céng shāng wù zhōng xīn de yòu biān.
餐厅在一层商务中心的右边。

A： At what time restaurant opens? Does it have western food?
cān tīng shénma shíhou kāi? yǒu méi yǒu xī cān?
餐厅什么时侯开？　那儿有没有西餐？

B： Restaurant opens every day from 6'O clock in the morning to 11'O clock in the night.
cān tīng měi tiān zǎo shang lìu diǎn dǎo wǎn shang shí diǎn.
餐厅每天早上六点到晚上十二点。

B： It also has western food.
tā yě yǒu xī cān.
它也有西餐。

A： Thanks for the entire introduction you gave. Good-bye.
xiè xiè nín de jiè shào. zàijiàn.
谢谢您的介绍。再见。

B： You need not to mention. Good-bye.
bú yòng kè qi. zàijiàn
不用客气。再见。

chéng chūzū qìchē

乘出租汽车

Boarding a Taxi

Dialogues:
huì huà:
会话：

A： Hello, is it a taxi stand?
Wèi, shì chūzū qìchē zhān ma?
喂， 是出租汽车站吗？

B： Yes it is, do you want a taxi?
shì, nín yào chē ma?
是， 您要车吗？

A： Yes, I want a taxi.
Duì, wǒ yào yí liàng chē.
对， 我要一辆车。

B： Ok. Where are you?
hǎo. nín zài nǎr?
好。 您在哪儿?

A： I am in room no. 212 of Beijing hotel. I am Mr. Kumar.
zài běi jīng fàn diàn, èr yāo èr fángjiān. wǒ jiào kǔ mǎ ěr xiān sheng.
在北京饭店， 212 房间。我叫苦马尔 先生.

B： Where do you want to go?
nín yào dào nǎr qù?
您要到哪儿去?

A： I will first go to Indian Embassy, then go to Capital Airport and Beijing University.
wǒ xiān qù yìn dù dà shǐ guǎn, zài qù shǒu dū jī chǎng hé běi jīng dàxuě.
我先去印度大使馆，再去首都机场和北大
（北京大学）

B： Do you want it immediately.
nín mǎ shàng jìu yào ma?
您马上就要吗？

A： No, not now, please come tomorrow morning at 9'Oclock.
bù shì mǎ shàng yào, qǐng míng tiān shàngwu jǐu diǎn lái.
不是马上要，请明天上午九点来。

B： Ok. Tomorrow morning at 8.30 car will be waiting for you at the main gate of the hotel.
xíng. míng tiān shàngwu bā diǎn zài fàn diàn de mén kǒu děng nín.
行。明天上午八点半车在饭店的门口等您。

A： Good. Give me the cart no please.
hǎo ba. qǐng nín gěi wǒ qìchē hàomǎ.
好吧！　请您给我汽车号码。

B： Most probably it will be 2128. is it ok?
dà gài shì èr yāo èr bā. kě yi ma?
大概 2128 号码。可以吗？

A：Ok. See you tomorrow.
kě yi. míng tiān jiàn.
可以。明天见。

B：Thanks. See you tomorrow.
xiè xiè! míng tiān jiàn.
谢谢！ 明天见。

duì huàn wài bì

兑换外币

Changing Foreign Currency

Dialogues:

huì huà:

会话:

A: Sir, I have some Indian Rupees that I would like to change to Renminbi.
xiān sheng, wǒ yào yìxiē yìn dù lú bǐ xiăng huànchéng rén mín bì.
先生，我有一些印度卢比想换成人民币。

B: Ok. How much do you want change?
Hăo ba! nín yào huàn duō shăo?
好巴！ 您要换多少？

A: Twenty eight thousand five hundred Rupees (Rs.28, 500).
liăng wàn bā qiān wŭ băi lú bǐ.
两万八千五百卢比（Rs.28, 500）。

B: Please fill first this exchange form, and then give me your passport.
Qǐng xiān tián yì zhāng duì huàn dān, zài gěi wǒ nín de hù zhào.
请先填一张兑换单，再给我您的护照。

A: Excuse me; what is the exchange rate, of Indian Rupees to Renminbi today?
qǐng wèn, jīn tiān de lú bǐ hé rén mín bì de duì huàn lu shì duō shǎo?
请问，今天的卢比和人民币的兑换率是多少？

B: Today the exchange rate of every 1 Renminbi is 5.8 Indian Rupees (01 RMB = 5.8 RS).
jīn tiān rén mín bì hé lú bǐ de duì huàn lu shì yī bǐ wǔ diǎn bā.
今天人民币和卢比的兑换率是一比五点八。

A: Thank you! Here is the exchange form and my passport.
xiè xiè! gěi nín duì huàn dān hé wǒ de hù zhào.
谢谢！给您兑换单和我的护照。

B: Please wait for a while.
Qǐng nín děng yì hui r.
请您等一会儿。

A: Fine. I am not busy.
xíng. *bù máng.*
行。不忙。

B: Your Twenty eight thousand five hundred Rupees (Rs.28, 500) has been exchanged to. Five thousand Renminbi (5,000 RMB). Please check and calculate it at once.
Nín de liǎng wàn bā qiān wǔ bǎi lú bǐ yī gòng huànchéng le wǔ qiān rén mín bì. Qǐng nín diàn yí xià.
您的两万八千五百卢比一共换成了五千人民币（**RMP.5000)**。请您点一下。

A: Ok. Thank you very much.
Hǎo le. xiè xiè nín.
好了。谢谢您。

zài yóu jú

在邮局

At the Post Office

Dialogues:

huì huà:

会话：

A: Sir, this is the first time I am mailing letter in China, and I don't know how much stamp to stick. Please help me.
xiān sheng, wǒ shì dì yī cè zài zhōng guó jì xìn, bù zhī dào yòng duō shǎo qián de yóupiào, qǐng nín bāng zhù wǒ.
先生，我是第一次在中国寄信，
不知道用多少钱的邮票，请您帮助我。

B: Ok. Where do you want to mail these letters?
Hǎo. nín zhè ji fēng xìn jì dào nǎr qù?
好。您这几封信寄到哪儿去？

A: This letter is to be mailed within the city; this one to Shanghai; and these two are sent to India.
zhè fēng xìn jì dào shì nèi, zhè fēng xìn jì dào Shànghǎi, zhè liǎng fēng shì yìndù de.
这封信寄到市内，这封信寄到上海，
这两封是印度的。

B: The letter to be posted within the City only needs a 1 Mao stamp.
shì nèi de xìn tiē yì máo qián yóupiào jìu xíng le.
市内的信贴一毛钱邮票就行了。

B: One sent to Shanghai needs 2 Mao stamp.
jì dào Shànghǎi de tiē liǎng máo qián yóupiào.
寄到上海的贴两毛钱邮票。

B: These letters to be posted abroad first let me weigh them.
zhè liǎng fēng jì dào guó wài de xìn, wǒ lái yāo yì yāo zhòng liàng.
这两封寄到国外的 信，我来约一约重量。

A: Fine.
Xíng.
行。

B: I weighed them. This letter sent to India is not overweight, just paste 2Yuan stamp.
wǒ yāo guò le, zhè fēng jì dào yìndù de méi chāo liàng, tiē liǎng kuài qián yóupiào.
我约过了，这封寄到印度的没超量，
贴两块钱邮票。

B: Another letter exceeds the weight; paste 2Yuan and 90 Fen.
bié de xìn chāo liàng le, tiē liǎng kuài jiǔde yóupiào.
别的信超量了，贴两块九 的邮票。

A: When will the letters from abroad reach India?
guó wài de xìn shénma shí hou dào yìndù?
国外的信什么时候到印度？

B: Almost ten days.
dà gài shí tiān.
大概十天。

A: Ok. How much is altogether?
Hǎo le. yí gòng duōshao qián?
好了。一共多少钱?

B: Altogether 5.2 Yuan.
yí gòng wǔ kuài liǎng máo.
一共五块两毛。

A: I am giving you 6 Yuan.
Gěi nín lìu kuài qián.
给您六块钱。

B: I am returning you 8 Mao.
Zhǎo nín bā máo.
找您八毛。

A: Ok. Thank you.
Hǎo le. xiè xiè.
好了。谢谢。

B: No needs to thank. Welcome you again.
bú yòng xiè. huānyíng nín zài lái.
不用谢。欢迎您再来。

cān guān péngyou jiā

参观朋友家

Visiting Friend's Place

Dialogues:

huì huà:

会话：

A: Mr. Wang is at home?
Wáng xiān sheng zài jiā ma?
王先生在家吗？

B: Yes he is. Who are you?
Zài. Nín shì shéi ya?
在。您是谁呀？

A: I am his friend from India.
wǒ shì cóng yìn dù lái de tā de péngyou.
我是从印度来的他的朋友。

C: (Mr. Wang). Aah. Mr. Kumar! Welcome.
(Wáng xiān sheng). à kǔ mǎ ěr xiān sheng! Huānyíng nín guāng lín!
（王先生）。啊苦马尔先生！欢迎您光临。

B: Please come in! Please be seated.
qǐng jìn lái ba! qǐng zuò.
请进来吧！请座。

A: Thank you.
xiè xiè.
谢谢！

C: When did you reach China?
Nín shénma shíhou dào le zhōng guó?
您什么时侯到了中国？

A: Last month I reached China, but yesterday I came to Shanghai.
Wǒ shàng gē yuè dào le zhōng guó, dàn shì zuó tiān lái shànghǎi le.
我上个月到了中国，但是昨天来上海了。

C: Have you come for leisure tour or for doing business?
Nín shì lái lǚ xíng hái shì lái zuò shēng yi de?
您是来旅游还是来做生意的？

A: This time I came for business.
Zhè cè wǒ shì lái shēng yi gàn de.
这次我是来生意干的。

C: That's Very good. Would you like to drink Coffee or Tea?
Hěn hǎo! nín yào hē kā fēi hái shì hē chá?
很好！ 您要喝咖啡还是喝茶？

A: I am very much fond of drinking your country's Jasmine Tea.
Wǒ hěn xǐ huan hē nǐmen zhōng guó de mòlǐ huāchá.
我很喜欢喝你们中国的茉莉茶。

A: I specially bought these gifts for children.
Zhè jiàn lǐ wù shì wǒ tè yì sóng gěi háize men de.
这些件礼物是我特意送给孩子们的。

C: It's all right. Today will together go for eating Indian supper.
bíe kè qi. Jīn tiān wǒmen yì qǐ chī yìn dù wăn fàn.
别客气。今天我们一起吃印度晚饭。

C: Here we have one very good Indian restaurant.
Zhè lǐ yǒu yì gē fēi cháng hăo de yìn dù fàn diàn.
这里有一个非常好的印度饭店。

A: That's well said!
Zhè hăo shuō ba!
这好说吧！

C: When will you depart from Shanghai?
Nín shénma shí hou lí kāi shànghăi?
您什么时侯离开上海？

A: Tomorrow early morning I am going to Guang Zhou by plane.
Ming tiān zăo shàng zuò fēi jī qù Guăng Zhōu shì.
明天早上坐飞机去广州市。

A： It's already too late, I will leave now.
xiàn zài shí jiān bù zăo le, wŏ zŏu ba.
现在时间不早了，我走吧。

C: Ok. Wish you would be having a pleasant traveling in China. See you.
Hăo. yuàn wàng nín de zhōng guó lǚ xíng yú kuài. Zài jiàn.
好。愿望您的中国旅行愉快。再见。

A: Thank you. If it is convenient, I welcome you to India. See you.
xiè xiè. Rúguŏ yŏu fāng biàn de huà, wŏ huānyíng nín yìn dù lái. Zài jiàn.
谢谢。如果有方便的话，我欢迎您到印度来。再见。

zài càn tīng

在餐厅

At the Restaurant

Dialogues:

会话:

A: Please come in! Please come in.
qǐng jìn! qǐng jìn!
请进！ 请进！

B: Do you have the seats for two?
Nǐmen yǒu liǎng gè rén de wéi zi ma?
你们有两个人的位子吗？

A: Yes. Please follow me. Please be seated here.
Yǒu. qǐng gēn wǒ lái. Qǐng zuò zhè li .
有。请跟我来。请座这里。

B: Thank you.
xiè xiè.
谢谢！

A: You would like to havc Chinese food or Western food?
Nín yào zhōng càn hái shì xī càn?
您要中餐还是西餐？

B: What is the most famous Chinese food you have?
Nǐmen de zuì yǒu míng de zhōng càn shì shénma?
你们的最有名的中餐是什么？

A: The most famous Chinese food is Sichuan cuisine's "Chicken with special hot sauce".
zuì yǒu míng de zhōng càn shì sìchuān cài de "guài wèi jī".
最有名中餐是四川菜的"怪味鸡"。

B: Please bring one plate of "Chicken with special hot sauce".
Qǐng nǐ lái yī pán "guài wèi jī".
请你来一盘"怪味鸡"。

A: Apart from Sichuan cuisine, what else do you want?
Chú le sìchuān cài yǐ wài, hái yào shénma?
除了四川菜以外，还要什么？

B: We would also like to have Chicken noodles.
hái yào jī ròu chǎo miàn.
还要鸡肉炒面。

A: What would you like to drink?
Nǐn hē diǎr shénma?
您喝点儿什么?

B: Do you serve (have) beer here?
Zhè lǐ yǒu méi yǒu pí jǐu?
这里有没有啤酒?

A: Yes.
Yǒu.
有。

B: Please also bring two bottles of beers.
Qǐng yě lái liǎng píng pí jǐu.
请也来两瓶啤酒。

A: Kindly wait for a moment, I will bring it immediately.
Qǐng shāo děng yī huìr, wǒ mǎ shàng lái le.
请稍等一会儿，我马上来了。

kàn bìng

看病

Seeing a Doctor

Dialogues:
huì huà:
会话：

A: Doctor, I don't feel very well.
Yī sheng, wǒ juéde bù shūfu.
医生，我觉得不舒服。

B: What's the matter?
Nǐ zěnma bù shūfu ya?
你怎么不舒服呀？

A: Yesterday my nose started to run, and now I have got a headache.
Zuótiān wǒ kāishǐ liú bítì, xiàn zài juéde tóu téng.
昨天我开始流鼻涕，现在觉得头疼。

B: Is your throat paining?
Hóu lóng téng ma?
喉咙疼吗？

A: Yes it is paining, also got a fever.
Téng, hái yǒu fāshāo.
疼，还有发烧。

B: Here's a prescription; take some medicine and rest. After few days you will be all right.
Zhè shì yàofāng; chī diǎr yào, xiūxi, xiūxi. Guò jǐ tiān jiù hǎo le.
这是 药方；吃点儿药，休息休息。
过几天就好了。

A: Ok. Thanks.
Hǎo. xiè xiè.
好，谢谢。

B: You are welcome.
bù xiè.
不谢。

zài shì chăng

在市场

At the Market

Dialogues:
huì huà:
会话：

A: Aah Mr. Kumar! Hello, are you busy?
à kŭ mă ĕr xiān sheng! nĭ hăo, nĭ máng ma?
啊，苦马尔先生！ 你好，你忙吗？

B: Yes. I am going to the nearby Supermarket for buying few clothes.
duì. wŏ qù fùjìn de chāojí shì chăng măi yī xiē yīfu.
对。我去附近的超级市场买一些衣服。

A: I am also planning to go there. Will go together, is it fine?
wŏ xiăng qù. zánmen yìqĭ zŏu, hăo ma?
我也想去。咱们一起走，好吗？

B: Ok.
hǎo.
好。

C: (Service boy at the shop) Hello gentlemen. What do you want?
(shāngdiàn de fúwùyùan) nǐn hǎo xiān sheng men. Nǐmen yào shénma?
（商店的服务员）您好先生们。你们要什么？

B: I want to buy few clothes. Let me see that shirt please.
wǒ yào mǎi yī xiē yīfu. lái wǒ kàn nà jiàn chènyì.
我要买一些衣服。来我看那件衬衣。

C: This one? How is it?
zhè jiàn ma? Nǐ kàn, zěnmeyàng?
这件吗？ 你看，怎么样？

B: Colour is fine but comparatively big, I don't want this one.
Yánsè hǎo, dànshì bǐ jiào dà, bú yào zhè jiàn.
颜色好，但是比较大，不要这件。

C: You see this one, how is it?
Nǐ kàn zhè jiàn, zěnmeyàng?
你看这件，怎么样？

B: Colour is fine; design is also good-looking, not big and not small, I will buy this one.
Yánsè hǎo, shèjì yě hen hǎo, bú dà, yě bù xiǎo, wǒ yào mǎi zhè jiàn.
颜色好，设计也很好，不大，也不小，
我要买这件。

C: What else do you want?
hái yào shénma?
还要什马？

B: Also want two trousers.
hái yào liǎng jiàn kùze.
还要两件裤子。

B: One of white colour and one of black colour.
yī jiàn bái de, yī jiàn hēi yánsè de.
一件白的，一件黑颜色的。

C: How are these one?
Zhè xiē zěnmeyàng?
这些怎么样？

B: It seems ok. Altogether how much?
hái kěyi. yīgòng duòshao qián?
还可以。一共多少钱？

C: Altogher 260 RMB.
Yīgòng liăng băi lìu shí rén mín bì.
一共两百六十人民币。

B: Here is 300 RMB.
Gěi nǐ sān băi rén mín bì.
给你三百人民币。

C: Returning you 40 kuai. Good buy.
zhào nǐ sì shí kuài. Zài jiàn.
找你四十块。再见。

B: Good buy.
Zài jiàn.
再见。

Tán guójí

谈国籍

Discussing Nationality

Dialogues:
huì huà:
会话：

A: Excuse me, what's your nationality?
Qǐng wèn nín shì nă guó rén?
请问您是哪国人？

B: I am an Indian.
Wŏ shì yìn dù rén?
我是印度人。

A: In India where did you come from?
nín shì cóng yìn dù de shénme dìfang lái de?
您是从印度的什么地方来的？

B: I come from New Delhi
Cóng xīn déli lái de.
从新德里来的。

A: Is she also an Indian?
Tā yě shì yìn dù rén ma?
她也是印度人吗？

B: No, she is not. She is from Thailand and she's my wife.
Bú shì, tā shì Tàiguó rén, wǒ de tàitai.
不是，她是泰国人，我的太太。

A: How do you do? Did you come by plane?
Nǐ hǎo. nǐmen shì zuò fēi jī lái de?
你好。你们是坐飞机来的吗？

B: No. We came by train.
Bú shì, shì zuò huǒ chē lái de.
不是，是坐火车来的。

A: Can you speak English?
Nǐ huì shuō yīng yǔ ma?
你会说英语吗？

B: Yes, only a bit.
Huì yìdiǎnr.
会一点儿。

Dìngpiào.

订票

Booking Tickets

Dialogues:

huì huà:

会话：

A: Sir, I would like to reserve two plane tickets.
Xiānsheng, wǒ yào yùdìng liǎng zhāng fēijī piào.
先生，我要预订两张飞机票。

B: Where are you going?
Nín yào qù nǎr?
您要去哪儿？

A: India, New Delhi.
Yìndù, xīn déli.
印度，新德里。

B: Which day's ticket you want to book?
Nǐn yào dìng nǎ tiān de piào?
您要订哪天的票？

A: I would like to book a ticket for the 5th of this month.
Wǒ xiǎng dìng běn yuè wǔ hào de.
我想订本月五号的。

B: Do you want to book Air China or Air India?
Nǐn shì dìng zhōngguó guójí hángkōng gōng sī de, háishì yìndù guójí hángkōng gōng sī de?
您是订中国国际航空公司的，
还是印度国际航空公司的？

A: Air India.
Dìng yìndù guójí hángkōng gōng sī de.
订印度国际航空公司的

B: What class do you want?
Nǐn dìng nǎ zhǒng cāng?
您订哪种舱？

A: Economy class.
Jīngjì cāng.
经济舱。

B: O.K. please comes two days ahead to pick up the tickets.
Hǎo, qíng nǐn tíqián liǎngtiān lái qǔ pìao.
好，请您提前两天来取票。

A: Do you accept credit cards?
Xìnrèn kǎ kěyǐ ma?
信任卡可以吗?

B: Yes, we do.
kěyǐ.
可以。

A: What do I need to bring along when I come to pick up the tickets?
qǔ pìao shí yào dài shénme ne?
取票时要带什么呢?

B: Bring your passport and money.
Dài nǐn de hù zhào hé qián.
带您的护照和钱。

A: Thank you.
Xiè xiè.
谢谢。

B: You are welcome.
Bié kèqi.
别客气。

Tán tiānqì

谈天气

Talking About the Weather

Dialogues:

Huì huà:

会话：

A: Where do you live?
Nǐ zhù zài nǎer?
你住在哪儿？

B: I live in Beijing.
wǒ zhù zài Běijīng.
我住在北京。

A: How is the whether there?
Nàer de tiān qì zěnmeyàng?
那儿的天气怎么样？

B: Weather is very good.
Nàer de tiān qì hěn hǎo.
那儿的天气很好。

A: How many seasons are there in one year?
Yī nián yǒu jǐ gè jì jié?
一年有几个季节？

B: There are four seasons in a year:
Yī nián yǒu sì gè jì jié:
一年有四个季节：

C: Spring, summer, autumn and winter.
chūn tiān, xià tiān, qīu tiān hé dōng tiān.
春天，夏天，秋天 和 冬天。

A: How is the whether in spring?
chūn tiān tiān qì zěnmeyàng?
春天天气怎么样？

B: Weather in spring is very comfortable.
chūn tiān tiān qì hěn shūfu.
春天天气很舒服。

A: How is the weather in summer?
xià tiān tiān qì zěnmeyàng?
夏天天气怎么样？

B: Summer is comparatively hot.
xià tiān tiān qì bǐjiào rè.
夏天天气比较热。

A: How is the weather in autumn?
qīu tiān tiān qì zěnmeyàng?
秋天天气怎么样？

B: Autumns are the best. Weather is very pleasant, not very cold yet not very hot.
qīu tiān zuì hǎo. tiān qì hěn liáng kuài, bù lěng yě bù rè.
秋天最好。天气很凉快，不冷也不热。

A: Very good, how is the weather in winters?
hěn hǎo, dōng tiān tiān qì zěnmeyàng?
很好，冬天天气怎么样？

B: The winters in Beijing are very cold.
Běi jīng de dōng tiān hěn lěng.
北京的冬天很冷。

A: It is not bad to live in Beijing.
zhù zài Běi jīng búcuò.
住在北京不错。

Yāo qǐng

邀请

Invitations

Dialogues:
huì huà:
会话：

A: Mr. Kumar, are you and your manager going to be free on this Saturday evening?
Kǔ mǎ ěr xiān sheng, zhè gè xīngqī lìu wǎn shàng, nǐ hé nǐ de jīng lǐ yǒu kòng ma?
苦吗尔 先生，这个星期六晚上，
你和你的经理有空吗？

B: Yes, we have. Why do you ask?
Yǒu kòng, shén me shì ya?
有空，什么事呀？

A: I would like to invite two of you to our house for Chinese food.
Wǒ xiǎng, qǐng nǐmen liǎng wèi dào wǒ jiā qù chī zhōng guó fàn.
我想请你们两位到我家去吃中国饭。

B: Oh, how nice. We love Chinese food. It is also very well known in India.
Tài hǎo le, wǒmen hěn xǐ huān chī zhōng fàn. Zhōng fàn zài yìn dù yě hěn yǒu míng.
太好了，我们很喜欢吃中菜。
中菜在印度也很有名。

B: By the way, is it some special occasion?
Duì le, yǒu shénme tè bié de shì qǐng kè ma?
对了，有什么特别的事请客吗？

A: No, nothing special.
Méi yǒu shénme tè bié de shì.
没有什么特别的事。

B: Will there be any other guests?
Hái yǒu bié de kè rén ma?
还有别的客人吗？

A: No.
Méi yǒu.
没有。

B: Excellent!
Hǎo jí le.
好极了。

A: O.K. then. Saturday night at 7 o'clock. Be sure to come.
Nàme xīngqī lìu wǎn shàng qī diǎn zhōng. Yí dìng lái ba.
那么星期六晚上七点钟。一定来吧。

B: Oh, we will. We certainly will.
Yí dìng, yí dìng.
一定，一定。

Zài Běi jīng lǚ xíng.

在北京旅行。

Traveling in Beijing

Dialogues:
huì huà:
会话：

A: Mr. Wang, I want to visit the places of tourist attraction in Beijing, but do not know the directions. Please help me a bit.
Wáng xīansheng, wǒ yào cānguān Běi jīng de jǐngdiǎn, dànshì bú zhìdào fāngwèi. Qíng nǐn bāng máng wǒ yī huìr.
王先生，我要参观北京的景点，
但是不知道方位。请您帮忙我一会儿。

B: No problem, please ask.
Méishì, méishì. Qíng nǐ wèn yī wèn.
没事，没事。请你问一问。

A: Is the Great Hall of People far from Imperial Palace?
Rénmín Dàhuìtáng lí Gùgōng yuǎn ma?
人民大会堂离故宫远吗？

B: Not far, it is very close from the Imperial Palace, just at the western side of the Tiananmen Square.
Bù yuǎn, lí Gùgōng hěn jìn, jìu zài Tiān' ānmén Guǎngchǎng xī bianr.
不远，离故宫很近，就在天安门广场西边儿。

A: Museum of Chinese History is also on the western side?
Zhōng guó Lìshǐ Bówùguǎn yě zài xī bianr ma?
中国历史博物馆也在西边儿吗？

B: No, Museum of the Chinese History and Museum of the Chinese Revolution is at the eastern side of the Tiananmen Square.
Bù, Zhōng guó Lìshǐ Bówùguǎn hé Zhōng guó Gémìng Bówùguǎn jìu zài Tiān' ānmén dōng bianr, Rénmín Dàhuìtáng duìmiàn.
不，中国历史博物馆和中国革命博物馆就在天安门东边儿，人民大会堂对面。

A: What about the Monument of the People's Heroes?
Rénmín Yīngxióng Jìnìan bèi ne?
人民英雄纪念碑呢？

B: It is located at the Centre of the Tiananmen Square, in front of Chairman Mao Zedong Memorial Hall.
Zài Tiān' ānmén Guǎng chǎng zhōngjiān, zài Máo Zhǔ xí Jìnìantáng qián bianr.
在天安门广场中间，在毛主席纪念堂前边儿。

A: Then, the front gate is at the backside of the Chairman Mao Zedong Memorial Hall. Is it correct?
Nàme, Qiánmén zài Máo Zhǔxí Jìnìantáng hòubianr duì bu duì?
那么，前门在毛主席纪念堂后边儿对不对？

B: Yes, all these places are very interesting, really worth to see.
Duì, zhè jì ge dìfang dōu hěn yǒu yìsì, zhí de kàn yi kàn.
对，这几个地方都很有意思，值得看一看。

Tán tán Yùn dòng

谈谈体育。

Talking About the Sports

Dialogues:
huì huà:
会话：

A: Is there any playground near your house?
Nǐ de jiā fùjìn yǒu cāochǎng ma?
你的家附近有操场吗？

B: Yes. The playground is very near from my house.
Yǒu. Cāochǎng lí wǒ jiā hěn jìn.
有。操场离我家很近。

A: I enjoy doing physical exercise.
Wǒ hěn xǐ huān duànliàn shēn ti.
我很喜欢锻炼身体。

B: Oh really! Everyday morning I go for physical exercise.
Shì ma! Wŏ mĕi tiān zăoshang dōu duànliàn shēn ti.
是吗！我每天早上都锻炼身体。

A: Do you also like sports?
Nĭ yĕ xĭhuān Yùn dòng ma?
你也喜欢运动吗？

B: Yes, I like sports very much.
Dùi, Wŏ hĕn xĭ huān Yùn dòng.
对，我很喜欢运动。

A: Do you play Basketball?
Nĭ dă bù dă lán qíu?
你打不打篮球？

B: No, I cannot play. But I play Badminton. What about you?
Bù, Wŏ bù huì dă. Dànshì wŏ dă yŭ máo qíu. Nĭ ne?
不，我不会打。但是我打羽毛球。你呢？

A: I am fond of cricket and swimming. Sometimcs, I also take part in competitions.
Wǒ xǐ huān bǎn qíu hé yóu yǒng. Wǒ yě cháng cháng cānjiā bǐ sài.
我喜欢板球和游泳。我也常常参加比赛。

B: Oh really! If it is convenient for you, from tomorrow we can together go to playground for physical excersise.
Shì ma! Rú guǒ yǒu fāngbiàn de huà, cóng míngtiān zánmen yīqǐ qù.
是吗？如果有方便的话，
从明天咱们可以一起去操场锻炼身体。

A: All right, from tomorrow we will go together. See you tomorrow.
Hǎo ba, cóng míngtiān yīqǐ qù. Míngtiān jiàn.
好 吧 ，从明天一起去。明天见。

B: See you tomorrow.
Míngtiān jiàn.
明天见。

Names of China's Provinces, Autonomous regions, Municipalities and China's Special Administrative Regions.

Provinces
省

1. Hebei Sheng 河北省.
2. Shanxi Sheng 山西省.
3. Liaoning Sheng 辽宁省.
4. Jilin Sheng 吉林省.
5. Heilongjiang Sheng 黑龙江省.
6. Jiangsu Sheng 江苏省.
7. Zhejiang Sheng 浙江省.
8. Anhui Sheng 安徽省.
9. Fujian Sheng 福建省.

10. Jiangxi Sheng 江西省.

11. Shandong Sheng 山东省.

12. Henan Sheng 河南省.

13. Hubei Sheng 湖北省.

14. Hunan Sheng 湖南省.

15. Guandong Sheng 广东省.

16. Hainan Sheng 海南省.

17. Sichuan Sheng 四川省.

18. Guizhou Sheng 贵州省.

19. Yunnan Sheng 云南省.

20. Shaanxi Sheng 陕西省.

21. Gansu Sheng 甘肃省.

22. Qinghai Sheng 青海省.

23. Taiwan Sheng 台湾省.

Autonomous Regions
自治区

1. Inner Mongolia Autonomous region
   内蒙古自治区。

2. Guangxi Zhuang Autonomous region
   广西壮族自治区。

3. Ningxia Hui Autonomous region
   宁夏回族自治区。

4. Tibet Autonomous region
   西藏自治区。

5. Xinjiang Uygur Autonomous region
   新疆维吾尔自治区。

Municipalities Directly Under Central Government
直辖市

1. Beijing Municipality
   北京市。
2. ChongqingMunicipality
   重庆市。
3. Shanghai Municipality
   上海市。
4. Tianjin Municipality
   天津市。

Special Administrative Regions
特别行政区

1. Macao Special Administrative Region
   澳门特别行政区。

2. Hongkong Special Administrative Region
   香港特别行政区。

Name of Major Countries in Chinese

Asia	*Yà Zhōu*	亚洲
1. Afghanistan	*Ā Fù Hàn*	阿富汗
2. United Arab Emirates	*Ā lián Qíu*	阿联酋
3. Pakistan	*Bā jī sī tǎn*	巴基斯坦
4. Bhutan	*Bù dān*	不但
5. N.Korea	*Cháo Xiǎn*	朝鲜
6. S.Korea	*Hán Guó*	韩国
7. Kuwait	*Kē Wēi tè*	科威特
8. Malaysia	*Mǎ Lái Xiā yà*	马来西亚
9. Bangladesh	*Mèng Jiā Lā Guó*	孟加拉国
10. Myanmar	*Miǎn Diàn*	缅甸
11. Nepal	*Ní Bó ěr*	尼泊尔
12. Japan	*Rì Běn*	日本
13. Sri Lanka	*Sī Lǐ Lán kǎ*	斯里兰卡

14. Thailand	*Tài Guó*	泰国
15. Singapore	*Xīn Jiā pō*	新加坡
16. Iraq	*Yī Lā kè*	伊拉克
17. Iran	*Yī Lǎng*	伊朗
18. Israel	*Yi Sè Liè*	以色列
19. India	*Yìn Dù*	印度
20. Indonesia	*Yìn Dù Ní Xī yà*	印度尼西亚
21. Vietnam	*Yuè Nán*	越南
22. China	*Zhōng Guó*	中国

Europe	***ōu Zhōu***	欧洲
1. Austria	*Ào Dì Lì*	奥地利
2. Belgium	*Bǐ Lì Shí*	比利时
3. Poland	*Bō Lán*	波兰
4. Denmark	*Dān Mài*	丹麦
5. Germany	*Dé Guó*	德国
6. Russia	Ē *Guó*	俄国
7. France	*Fá Guó*	法国

8. Netherlands	*Hé Lán*	荷兰
9. Romania	*Luó Mă Ní yà*	罗马尼亚
10. Portugal	*Pú Táo yá*	葡萄牙
11. Sweden	*Ruì Diăn*	瑞典
12. Switzerland	*Ruì Shì*	瑞士
13. Spain	*Xī Bān Yá*	西班牙
14. Greece	*Xī Là*	希腊
15. Italy	*Yì Dà lì*	意大利
16. United Kingdom	*Yīng Guó*	英国

Africa	***Fēi Zhōu***	非洲
1. Algeria	*Ā ĕr Jí Lì Yà*	阿尔及利亚
2. Egypt	*Āi Jí*	埃及
3. Ghana	*Jiā Nà*	加纳
4. Zimbabwe	*Jīn Bā Bù Wéi*	津巴布韦
5. Kenya	*Kĕn Ní Yà*	肯尼亚
6. Mali	*Mă Lĭ*	马里
7. Mauritius	*Máo Lĭ Qíu sī*	毛里求斯

8. South Africa	*Nán Fēi*	南非
9. Nigeria	*Ní Rì Lì yà*	尼日利亚
10. Sudan	*Sū Dān*	苏丹

Oceania	***Dà Yáng Zhōu***	大洋洲
1. Australia	*Āo Dà lì yà*	澳大利亚
2. New Zealand	*Xīn xī lán*	新西兰

North America	***Běi Měi***	北美
1. Canada	*Jiā Ná dà*	加拿大
2. United States	*Měi Guó*	美国
3. Mexico	*Mò xī gē*	墨西哥

South America	***Nán Měi***	南美
1. Argentina	*Ā Gēn Tíng*	阿根廷
2. Brazil	*Bā xī*	巴西
3. Colombia	*Gē Lún Bǐ yà*	哥伦比亚
4. Venezuela	*Wěi Nèi ruì lā*	委内瑞拉
5. Chile	*Zhì Lì*	智利